可　　　　存　　　性
享　　　　佛　　之
等　　　　他　　內
消　　　　也
逢　　　　無
後　　　　缺

Dear Phil,
We hope you
enjoy this book.
Happy Birthday.
Love Rod, Clair & Victoria
xxx

THE
FIVE FOOT
ROAD

IN SEARCH OF A VANISHED CHINA

PREVIOUS PAGE: *New Year greeting poster, Dali*
ABOVE: *Boy in truck, Shanghai*
OPPOSITE PAGE: *Morrison in western China*

THE
FIVE FOOT
ROAD

IN SEARCH OF A VANISHED CHINA

Angus McDonald

Angus&Robertson
An imprint of HarperCollins*Publishers*

Permissions

Grateful acknowledgement to A & C Black (Publishers) Ltd., London, for permission to quote the translation of the poem by Sun Ranweng on page 103 which appears in their *Blue Guide: China* by Frances Wood © 1992.

Thanks, too, to Bertil Lintner for permission to reproduce the extract from his paper 'The Politics of the Drug Trade in Burma' presented at the conference '*The State, Order and Prospects for Change in Burma*' at Griffith University, Brisbane, in December 1992, which appears on pages 151 and 152, and for other advice and information.

Angus&Robertson
An imprint of HarperCollins*Publishers*, Australia

First published in Australia in 1995

Copyright © Angus McDonald 1995

HarperCollins*Publishers*
25 Ryde Road, Pymble, Sydney NSW 2073, Australia
31 View Road, Glenfield, Auckland 10, New Zealand
77–85 Fulham Palace Road, London W6 8JB, United Kingdom
Hazelton Lanes, 55 Avenue Road, Suite 2900, Toronto, Ontario M5R 3L2
and 1995 Markham Road, Scarborough, Ontario M1B 5M8, Canada
10 East 53rd Street, New York NY 10032, USA

National Library of Australia Cataloguing-in-Publication data:
McDonald, Angus, 1962–.
The five foot road: in search of a vanished China.
Includes index.
ISBN 0 207 18670 7.
1.McDonald, Angus, 1962– — Journeys — China. 3.China — Description and travel. I.Title.
915.10459

Cover photograph by Angus McDonald

Printed in Hong Kong

9 8 7 6 5 4 3 2 1
99 98 97 96 95

ACKNOWLEDGEMENTS

While I went off and had all the fun, many friends and supporters gave generously of their valuable time, energy and resources because they believed in the idea. Without their help, this book would not exist.

Greatest thanks are due to those companies whose support, financial or in kind, made the expedition possible. The chief sponsor and provider of most of the finance was Emery Coatings, on the inspiration of Managing Director Julian Emery. Olex Cables provided additional financial support, and thanks are due to Managing Director Ian Campbell. Thai Airways International, whose comfortable and reliable flights service every destination I needed to reach by air, gave me a generous discount on my fares, and particular thanks are due to Sue Larsen and Julie Abbott of that company. David Cumming Colour House in Sydney developed my films free of charge and stored them until my return, as well as performing other favours too numerous to list. A heartfelt thanks to David and Marie.

Many others helped in a variety of ways. They are, in no particular order, Mike Jones and the Australia–China Chamber of Commerce and Industry of New South Wales, the State Library of New South Wales, the good folk of the Thai–Yunnan Border Project at the Australian National University, Judith Jaffe, Louise Williams, Pam Gutman, Sorrel Wilby, Hugh and Marney Dunn, Kate and Charles Qin, Tanya and Wei Shaw, Angela Parker and James Mort, Jon Philp and Steve Robinson of the Australian Embassy in Rangoon, Htay Aung of the Burmese Directorate of Hotels and Tourism, Lo Hui-min, and everyone who read the finished manuscript and gave valuable suggestions for modifications. Lastly, but only chronologically, thanks to my editor, Sue Grose-Hodge, for her tolerance of an artistic temperament, and the rest of the team at HarperCollins, whose ideas for making this book were never at the expense of my own.

I apologise to anyone I may have inadvertently left off the list. All opinions and any errors of fact are, of course, entirely my own.

CONTENTS

中国

Prologue
8

CHAPTER ONE

An Australian in China
The Life and Times of
G.E. Morrison
11

CHAPTER TWO

Paris of the Orient, Sodom of the East
Shanghai
22

CHAPTER THREE

The Long River
Shanghai to Wuhan
38

CHAPTER FOUR

Temples of Cement
The Yangtze Gorges
46

CHAPTER FIVE

A Depressing Fever-stricken City
Chongqing
60

CHAPTER SIX
Electric Shadows
Chongqing to Kunming
71

CHAPTER SEVEN
The Pagodas and Lofty Temples of the Famous City
Kunming
86

CHAPTER EIGHT
The Goddess of Mercy
Kunming to Dali
105

CHAPTER ELEVEN
Monopoly Money
Rangoon
156

CHAPTER TWELVE
Slow Boat to Mandalay
Mandalay and Bhamo
173

CHAPTER NINE
The Southern Silk Road
Dali to the Burma Border
125

CHAPTER TEN
Opium
Dali
147

Epilogue
187

Bibliography
190

Index
191

PROLOGUE

The flight from Hong Kong took a couple of hours, and it was packed. By the time we circled Shanghai the sun was long gone, the city below us a mosaic of little green, yellow and red lights stretching off in every direction to the horizon. We touched down and a small wave of humanity débouched into the fluorescent glare of the airport terminal. Middle-aged women in pyjamas and happy shoes carried jade carvings and elaborate mah-jong sets; middle-aged men in polyester suits carried bulging black briefcases; there were video recorders, CD players, golf clubs, Ray-Bans and cameras. A sign on a polished pillar told us, in English and Chinese, that smoking and spitting were prohibited. Next to me, one of the businessmen was lighting up.

My battered old backpack eventually appeared and I was on my way. I usually negotiate airports on autopilot these days, but after a few minutes wandering the reception hall I realised something was wrong. I fronted the hotel booking counter.

'Do you want to book a hotel?' asked three smartly dressed young men in unison.

'No, I just want to find the bank. I need some money.'

'The bank is closed,' said the smoothest of the three. 'But don't worry. I will change money for you. Six hundred yuan for $100.'

I know I look like a soft touch, but it usually takes a bit more than that. I heaved my luggage around for a few more minutes, refusing to believe that the money exchange could be closed when there were still international flights coming in. By now I had three pairs of young women trailing me about the terminal, asking me to change money. To save time, one of them eventually led me to the bank. It was, indeed, closed.

If years of travel in Asia has taught me one thing, it's that sometimes there's simply no avoiding getting ripped off. At such times it's usually better to just get it over with. More for the sake of formality than out of any real sense of doing something illegal, I ducked behind a kiosk with one of the girls while we did the deed. I handed over my crisp $50 bill and in return got some creased 100-*renminbi* notes. 'People's money', that means. Across the front, Mao Zedong, Zhou Enlai, Zhu De and some bloke I didn't recognise were lined up in stony profile, faces fixed on the glorious socialist future, blind eyes turned to the present it had become. Last time I'd been in China, six years before, even 50-yuan notes had been so rare most people had taken a second look before accepting them.

I walked outside and hailed a taxi. In the streets of Shanghai there seemed to be a million of them, and they were all red. Neon signs, shops, restaurants, street stalls, pedestrians, rickshaws, cars, trucks, great grimy articulated trolleybuses and an endless chaos of bicycles all seemed to have coagulated in a barely moving mass with no definable border between road and footpath, footpath and building. On the radio, an English DJ was slick-talking his way through the top forty. We passed a huge sign, blue letters on white, which said, 'A MORE OPEN CHINA AWAITS THE 2000 OLYMPICS.'

The drive downtown took about an hour. The cabbie had a little English. 'Been driving long?' I asked, hoping this time-honoured opening wouldn't be greeted with a groan of boredom.

'A few years,' he said. 'I left my job as a teacher to do this. It was good then. There weren't so many taxis. I could make as much in a month as I would in a year as a teacher. It was easy then, in the eighties. Now everyone wants to be a driver. Look how many there are! Sometimes it's impossible to get a fare.'

I remembered the China of 1984, where taxis were a rare sight. In those days they were big Datsun saloons, and you just about had to have an uncle in the Politburo to get a job driving one. Or to afford to take one, for that matter.

'And look at this,' he said, gesturing at two sheets of thick perspex that caged him in. One sheet was behind him, between the roof and the top of his seat; the other ran from the roof to the floor between the passenger and driver seats in the front, barely giving him room to manipulate the gearstick. It was the first thing I had noticed when I got in the car. 'Now every taxi must have one, by law.'

'What's it for?' I asked.

'Nowadays many poor people come to Shanghai from the country. They don't have work permits and they can't get jobs. Soon they run out of money. So some of them would hail a taxi, pull out a knife and rob the driver. A few drivers have been killed.'

We pulled up at a hotel in the heart of the city, a hotel that the backpacker guides list as one of the cheapest in town. The woman on reception looked up from her book with an irritated expression, and pointed at a price list. Rooms started at A$70 a night. I thought for a second I must have landed in Tokyo by mistake.

Another half hour in the cab and I was at another hotel, a big barn of a place on the outskirts of town whose polished granite lobby and crisp receptionists aroused fresh misgivings. But we struck a deal and I was shown to a room. Leaving behind the lobby, with its business centre full of IBMs and its shop full of Mars Bars and

Colgate, down cavernous corridors and up draughty staircases, the layers fast peeled back to reveal a more familiar China.

The carpets were threadbare and held decades of gunge. In my room, illuminated by about five 25-watt light fittings, there was lugubrious furniture, vast armchairs with lacy white antimacassars, a thermos of hot water decorated with a lurid painting of birds singing on a branch, and a table lamp of such heavy, horrendous Soviet ugliness that I was sorely tempted to souvenir it.

I tried the bathroom. The plug fitted. Socialism with Chinese characteristics.

I went to bed, and was soon sleeping a dreamless sleep. But not for long. That night, the phone rang three times, the receiver just about bouncing off the hook with an irritable mechanical jangle. Each time I picked it up, a torrent of high-pitched Chinese was shouted in my ear. As soon as I said, 'What?' the caller hung up.

I was back in China alright.

Quite a few years ago, when I was making a somewhat erratic study of Chinese history for an arts degree, a particular book used to catch my eye on my infrequent, usually panic-stricken visits to the echoing depths of the university library. The book was called *Morrison of Peking* and it was written by Cyril Pearl, a man about whom I knew nothing except for a vague memory that he used to tell risqué jokes on an obscure TV game show on Sunday nights in the early seventies. But it was one of those names that somehow sticks in your mind. So one day I picked up the book and leafed through it.

Author and friends in Gongshan, Yunnan

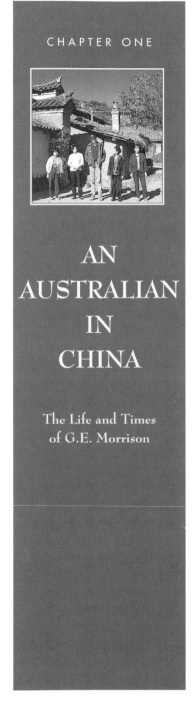

CHAPTER ONE

AN AUSTRALIAN IN CHINA

The Life and Times of G.E. Morrison

I remember taking note of the fact that the Morrison of the title was an Australian who'd had some claim to fame as a foreign correspondent in China around the turn of the century. There were a number of pictures in the book, but I can't say that the succession of black-and-white portraits of a square-jawed, steely-eyed man in Edwardian suits, from youth through to middle age, made any great impression on my memory. One image did stick, though. The caption said, 'Morrison, in Chinese dress, leaving Yunnan City during his walk across China in 1894'. Morrison stood in the centre, the only white man, in a Chinese cap and a long robe that fell almost to his feet. Under his arm was a black umbrella and on his face was the same look of relentless determination that featured in every other photo of him. On either side of him stood some ragged-looking Chinese men, a couple of them carrying loads slung from bamboo shoulder poles. I was vaguely intrigued, but I had a thesis to write and more than enough to read without distractions like this. So I put the book back on the shelf and didn't think about it again for ten years.

In 1991 I found myself in India for (I think) the fourth time, working on another research project. This time it was about Indian cinema, one of the more outlandish of the world's film industries, and certainly the biggest. After a year in India I completed my research and was invited to join an expedition to Mount Everest as photographer. I'd never held an ice axe in my life.

In April 1992 I sat at 6,000 metres (19,685 feet) at Camp One on Everest, with the jumbled sea of jagged seracs that is the Khumbu Ice Fall at my feet, and beyond it the perfect cone of Pumori peak, and beyond that the massive flanks of Cho Oyu, and beyond that and behind me and on every side as far as the eye could see the eternal and incomparable grandeur of the Himalayas glistening beneath a sky of rock-hard blue. I thought of the months of marshalling of arguments, of ordering of facts and statistics, of typing and footnoting and proofing and cross-checking, of writing and rewriting and reading and rereading that lay ahead of me before I could lay claim to a master's degree and finally acknowledged what I had already known instinctively for a long time: I was never going to be an academic. Any writer who's rubbed the magic lamp of India knows that the genie never really goes back into the bottle. It was time to find another lamp.

A familiar figure came into view and jolted me out of my reverie. It was Raymond Jacob, a powerfully built Indian clad in red Polartec, one of the strongest climbers on our team. He was ferrying a load up to Camp One, and would help me with the tricky descent back down the Ice Fall to Base Camp. I shouldered my pack and we set off, the hard ice crunching beneath our boots. Patiently, Raymond waited at the bottom of each descent as I struggled with ropes, crampons and karabiners, when at any moment the fierce rays of the mid-morning sun could have loosened one of the enormous blocks of ice that surrounded us, sending it crashing down to obliterate us without a trace. In a couple of hours we were back at Base, and the next day I left to return to Kathmandu.

A couple of weeks later I read in a Bombay newspaper that Raymond had died of exposure in a blizzard just a few metres short of Camp Four. So had our leader, D.T. Kulkarni. It was the end of the expedition. I was saddened, but somehow not shocked. Raymond and D.T. had known the risk they were taking in going up that mountain, and so had I. If someone asked me to do it again, I'd go tomorrow.

Back in Sydney, I got on with drafting, footnoting and proofing my thesis. Then one day my uncle, Hugh Dunn, himself a tireless traveller and scholar, and a former Australian ambassador to China, mentioned to me that this man Morrison had once trekked across China and Burma, starting from Shanghai and finishing in Rangoon. A few weeks later, I returned to my old haunt at Fisher Library, picked Cyril Pearl's book off the shelf, and sat down to read.

From the dust jacket I saw that Morrison, as the correspondent of *The Times* of London in Peking — Beijing — had probably been the most influential foreigner in China at the turn of the century, that he had witnessed and chronicled the last days of the Chinese Empire and the birth of the Chinese Republic and that his expertise had been sought by powerbrokers, presidents and diplomats, Chinese and Western alike. Then I opened the book and began to read. What follow here are just the most basic facts from what I read that day about the amazing life of George Ernest Morrison.

He was born in 1862 in Geelong, Australia, the son of Scots immigrants. His father was the headmaster of Geelong College and he grew up in that town. In 1878 he began keeping a diary, training himself into a habit of detailed observation that would last him the rest of his life. Among many other things, he recorded some stock-standard schoolboy daydreams about one day being a great explorer or a famous foreign correspondent.

The next year, on holiday after finishing school, he threw a few things into a knapsack and walked to Adelaide, more than 1,210 kilometres (752 miles) away, across sparsely inhabited and barely explored country. It was the height of summer and Morrison was alone. He reached Adelaide in six and a half weeks, on some days walking 56 kilometres (35 miles) in blistering heat. Similar exploits followed. The following summer, he bought himself a 4-metre (13-foot) canoe and paddled down the River Murray from Albury, on the Victoria–New South Wales border, to its mouth, 2,502 kilometres (1,555 miles) away in South Australia, the first person on record to do so. Then he walked back to Geelong.

A couple of years later, having been thrown out of the Faculty of Medicine at Melbourne University, when he scored less than 25% in one of his exams, he sailed the Pacific as a journalist investigating the trade in kanakas, islanders who were being used as virtual slave labour on Queensland sugar plantations. Three months later he walked back across Australia, crossing the continent from Normanton to Melbourne in 123 days, a distance of 3,288 kilometres (2,043 miles). He was alone, unarmed and had no compass. Somewhere between Winton and Cooper Creek, he turned twenty-one.

Soon afterwards, he led an expedition to New Guinea which ended in disaster: Morrison was speared in the face and stomach after taking a pot shot at a local. Sailing to Scotland for specialised medical treatment, he finally took his medical degree at Edinburgh University, and for the next four years alternately practised as a doctor and travelled in America, Europe and Africa.

In 1893 he made his first visit to Asia, the vast continent on our doorstep which white Australia has, since its foundation, regarded with a mixture of fascination, suspicion and, most commonly, sheer ignorance. He visited Hong Kong, the Philippines, China and Japan. Unable to find a job in Japan and fast running out of possessions he could pawn, he returned to Shanghai, where his mother telegraphed him £40.

And this was where it got really interesting.

From Shanghai, Morrison set out on what he would later describe as 'a quiet journey across China to Burma'. Beginning the journey by boat, he sailed 2,414 kilometres (1,500 miles) up the Yangtze River, through the heartland of China to the city of Chungking (now Chongqing). Leaving the river, he reverted to his favourite form of transport. He walked — or sometimes rode on ponies or mules or in sedan chairs — the rest of the way across China, another 2,414 kilometres to Burma. Greeted at the border by a garrison of British troops, he sailed down the Irrawaddy River to Mandalay, and from Mandalay he took a train to Rangoon. He then returned to Australia.

By Morrison's standards it might have been a quiet journey, but by any normal reckoning it was an epic. China at that time was an atrophied empire teetering on the brink of collapse, a revolution waiting to happen, a morass of corruption, rebellion, addiction, starvation and misery. In its interior, foreigners were a rarity — pale-skinned, blue-eyed devils regarded at once with wonder and fear, derision and hostility. In the decade before Morrison set out, there were regular anti-foreign riots along the Yangtze.

Morrison had traversed this vast land alone, without speaking a word of the language. He had almost drowned in the surging waters of the Yangtze Gorges; he had passed from the densely populated cities of the east to the remote backblocks of the south-west, where range piles upon range in a broken jumble of country that has caused conquerers from Kublai Khan to the Japanese Imperial Army to curse from the bottoms of their avaricious hearts. Finally, he had crossed into Burma over densely forested hills where gun-toting, sword-carrying tribespeople were a law unto themselves.

In February 1895 Morrison arrived in London clutching the manuscript of a book about the journey. It was called *An Australian in China* and it was published later that year, the only book he would ever write. Moberly Bell, the manager of *The Times*, read the book and invited Morrison to come and meet him. When Morrison sat down in his office, Bell offered him the job of Peking correspondent.

I had read enough. Leafing through the rest of the book, I saw that Morrison had worked for *The Times* for seventeen years. He had been wounded at the siege of the Peking legations — the Boxer Rebellion — and had written the officially accepted account of that episode in *The Times*. He had helped to provoke the Russo-Japanese War of 1904–5, and he helped to bring China into World War I. His last official post was political adviser to the President of the infant and fragile Chinese Republic. All very interesting, but I didn't take much of it in at the time; right then my head was swimming with the idea which had just hatched fully fledged inside it. Morrison had set out from Shanghai on 11th February 1894. It was now September 1992. I had just over a year to prepare to retrace Morrison's journey from Shanghai to Rangoon for its hundredth anniversary.

* * *

The concept was beautifully simple. I would take Morrison's book and try to visit every place he visited. I would compare the China he described in 1894 to the China of today. The concept was simple, yes — all I really had to do was buy a copy of his book and get going. But it was also vast. China since 1894 has been turned upside-down and shaken like a salt cellar with a blocked hole: it has endured two revolutions, two civil wars, an invasion and the madness of the Cultural Revolution. Last but not least has come a decade of economic development at breakneck pace, wreaking still more far-reaching change. In all likelihood, Morrison's China would have disappeared without a trace. And all this without even considering Burma, the biggest country in continental South-East Asia, an obscure land with a dark reputation.

On the other hand, one century, however tumultuous, is a blink of the eye for a civilisation with a continuous history of more than 3,000 years. Every society is a product of its past, and China's past is richer and longer than most. History, like memory, exists in the present, and only the past can give meaning to the present. Go looking for the one, and the other won't be far off.

And then there was Morrison. Who was this strange, complex paradox of a man? What drove him to these astonishing feats of physical endurance? How to reconcile his years of drifting with his later career, which was marked by a driving, almost ruthless ambition, and an ego to match? And what was his place in history? Was he just a Kiplingesque cliché, gathering fame and glory on the back of the colonial carve-up of China? Or was there more to him than that?

According to Pearl, he was a noble, larger-than-life hero, a paragon of journalistic integrity and a devotee of Chinese culture who built up one of the largest private collections of Western literature on Asia. But later I read a book called *Dragon Lady* — a re-evaluation of the life of China's infamous Empress Dowager, Cixi — which painted a darker portrait of the journalist. According to the author, Sterling Seagrave, Morrison as *Times* correspondent filed false or distorted reports on such pivotal events as the Boxer Rebellion. Some of the falsehoods were intentional, some merely careless, but because of their source they quickly took on the authority of historical fact. As a result of these distortions, which Seagrave claims Morrison made to further the interests of both the British Empire and his own career, an entire chapter of Chinese history has been misunderstood, and the very perception of Chinese society throughout the West has been skewed.

In his efforts to track down a motive for these wrongs, Seagrave has decided that Morrison was 'a lazy, self-indulgent man, intolerant, racist and unprincipled'. Yet seventy pages later he calls him 'a fundamentally moral and ethical man whose distortions were Olympian in their motivation'. What I was to make of all this, I wasn't quite sure. But between the accounts of the admiring Pearl and the indecisive Seagrave, there was a real human being somewhere, struggling to get out.

* * *

From another shelf in that vault-like library, my head swirling with images of bound feet and Mao suits, misty mountains and black bicycles, the Forbidden City and Tiananmen Square, I picked up a copy of *An Australian in China*. There, as the frontispiece, was the familiar photo of Morrison, captioned 'The author in Western China'. It had been taken in Yunnan City — modern-day Kunming — about halfway through the journey, by a man who had befriended Morrison there. His name was Jensen, and he was a Dane employed by the Chinese government to install telegraph lines in the country's south-west. Leafing through the book, I saw that it included about thirty illustrations, most of which were photos taken by Jensen of scenes along Morrison's route. Here was a picture of an elaborate and ancient city gate; there, a scene from a village. They were strong, technically competent photos, made by someone who knew what he was doing. Another idea exploded in my head: as I travelled, I would try and locate where these photos had been taken, and photograph whatever stood there now.

When I finished reading, I realised that this book was more than a mere travel account, entertaining though it was. It was a valuable historical document — a chronicle of a disappeared world, intimate and detailed. Morrison was one of the last witnesses to the old China — a millennia-old social system that was about to be swept away by decades of anarchy, war and revolution — and he had described that world in detail. The challenge would be to find how much of that China had survived into the late twentieth century.

The book also revealed much about the author. Dressed as a Chinese, even to the point of wearing a hat with a false queue (pigtail), travelling on foot and sleeping in grimy inns, tumbledown temples and simple farmhouses, Morrison had experienced China as few other Westerners of his time would have dared. In the cities, he had stayed with European or American missionaries — the real pioneers of Western travel in China — filling his notebooks with information about the road ahead and filling his belly with roast beef. But if Morrison was energetic and observant, he was also single-minded, opinionated and a bit of a loner. He could also be ungrateful, arrogant and tightfisted. If I was going to have him for a travelling companion, I realised, it was probably just as well that he was dead.

* * *

What kind of place was the China of 1894? Here are a couple of examples. The basic unit of currency was the *cash*, a round copper coin with a hole in the middle so it could be carried in strings. Exchange rates varied from one town to the next in a system of cumbersome, almost impenetrable complexity which Morrison devotes two pages of his book to describing. The Chinese had invented the coin, just as they'd invented the compass, the water wheel, gunpowder and the mechanical clock, but they were complacent pioneers. Innovation had once made the country strong but, by 1894, most Chinese technology was about as relevant as a suit of armour in a guerrilla war. Copper cash of the design used by Morrison first came into circulation during the Zhou period, possibly around the sixth century BC, and had been in continuous use ever since.

Then, in World War I, copper prices went through the roof and quantities of coins, some of them over 1,000 years old, were collected and melted down for export, notably to Japan. By the 1930s, an institution that had been a central feature of Chinese life for 2,500 years had vanished from the face of the earth. Modern Chinese coins are lightweight aluminium things, and there are few in circulation.

Another example. Between Chongqing in central China and Dali, 1,000 kilometres (621 miles) to the south-west, ran a highway that was laid out by the Qin dynasty — whose name, pronounced *Chin*, is the origin of the Western term 'China' — as part of a road-building program that was as crucial to the development of Chinese civilisation as Roman roads were to Europe. The road, a causeway designed for foot traffic, was known as the Five Foot Road (*Wuchidao*), so-called because in many places five feet was as wide as they could make it. When it was built in the third century BC this remarkable bit of engineering, which included many hanging galleries (wooden walkways banged into sheer cliffs through otherwise impassable gorges), had prised open the vast, rugged Yunnan –Guizhou Tableland like a can opener. The same route remains in use today, but it was a footpath until as late as 1938, when a motor road replaced it.

When Morrison travelled from Kunming to Dali, he followed this route, then the major artery of trade, thick with coolies and pack animals and the occasional sedan chair. In some places it was paved, in others it was just a dusty track winding up pine-covered hills and down dark gorges, its decay mirroring the decline of dynastic power. In 1894 Yunnan, China's sixth-biggest province, was only two decades away from secession.

This was the country that had long been accustomed to calling itself *Zhongguo* — the Middle Kingdom. The biggest country in Asia and the oldest surviving civilisation in the world, China had, perhaps understandably, come to see itself as the central power, the most sophisticated culture, sharing the globe with a few tribes of second-rate barbarians. Underpinned by the Confucian system of ethics, which taught reverence for the old and a disdain for innovation, Chinese society had atrophied to the point where little remained of its past strength save an unshakeable faith in its own superiority.

When Europeans began to arrive on the scene in numbers, about five centuries ago, their impact was minimal and they were simply regarded as another tribe of barbarians. But in the mid nineteenth century, with the industrial revolution surging ahead in Europe and North America and the 200-year-old Qing (or Manchu) dynasty at Peking fast running out of steam, the West would impact on China with a force that would shatter that ancient society beyond repair. And when a 2,000-year-old system binding together a population of about 400 million shatters beyond repair then, in a manner of speaking, all hell breaks loose.

In the first half of the nineteenth century, many Western businesspeople were dazzled by the potential that China represented. Here was the biggest market in the world, and it was virtually untapped. Dreaming a dream that should sound familiar enough even today, they believed that all they had to do was to gain access to that market, and riches would automatically follow. China was also the sole supplier of commodities which the West at that time craved, such as tea and silk. The problem was, China wanted nothing to do with these uncouth, unwashed, hairy merchants. To China's imperial élite, the products of Western industry were bizarre, incomprehensible, fatuous. The Middle Kingdom required nothing that it could not supply for itself.

But there was a simple enough solution to that.

The British possessed one thing in quantity for which a demand could soon be created: opium. By the 1840s large numbers of Chinese of all classes had become addicted to the drug, which was imported illegally but cheaply from British India.

When the Chinese authorities tried to clamp down on it, the foreigners responded with the overwhelming might of their modern navies in two conflicts that have become known as the Opium Wars.

By the time the smoke had cleared, the Western powers had extracted major concessions from the Chinese, including the right to set up their own trading enclaves in a number of coastal cities, and to travel at will in the interior of the country. The consequences were colossal. China was flooded with cheap manufactured goods from the West, destroying traditional crafts and throwing tradespeople out of work by the million. The country's silver reserves were drained to pay for the imports, causing high inflation. And the government at Peking had been comprehensively humiliated by barbarians they considered their inferiors. The results were a deeply-felt resentment of the West, suffering and deprivation on a massive scale and, ultimately, revolution.

Here's another example from Morrison. When he arrived at Yunnan City (now Kunming) and fell in with Jensen, the engineer, the Dane told Morrison that the installation of the telegraph had met with resistance from villagers because it was believed that the lines would interfere with the *fengshui* of the region — that is, according to traditional belief, they would disrupt the disposition of the elements and divert good fortune away from the area. As a consequence, villagers had been cutting down telegraph poles and selling the wire. To solve the problem, the local magistrate had arrested a couple of villagers, beaten a confession out of them and cut their ears off. 'No poles have been cut down since,' wrote Morrison.

In fact, such problems were not so simply solved. Five years later, in 1899, northern China erupted in a rebellion that was led by a group called the Fists of Righteous Harmony. Better known to us as the Boxers, this secret society was aggressively anti-foreign. Among the many grievances on which they drew for support was the laying of railway lines by Western contractors and the building of churches by Western missionaries in places where it was believed the fengshui would be disturbed. Railways had also deprived boatpeople, porters and others whose livelihoods depended on traditional transport, of a living. The Boxers invaded churches and massacred missionaries and Chinese Christians, finally besieging the diplomatic legations of Peking in the controversial episode which would make Morrison's reputation as a journalist.

By the time an international force had relieved the legations, looted the city and driven the imperial court from the capital, the course of history had changed. Retreat into the past was no longer an option. Twelve years later, the Qing dynasty collapsed. A revolution had begun.

Thirty-seven years of turmoil followed: China split up into fiefdoms controlled by warlords and was subsequently ruled by a weak and corrupt Republican (Guomindang) government obsessed with trying to eradicate the communists, who had grown rapidly since the Party's birth in 1921. Then the Japanese invaded, gaining control of the country's fertile and populous eastern half for the best part of a decade. Four more years of civil war followed, but in China the final victory always goes to the faction that can mobilise the country's vast peasantry behind it. In 1949 China at last had a new 'dynasty' — the Communist Party — with a powerful new 'emperor' at its head.

* * *

That's history too, these days. Mao's ideas have been largely abandoned, and as I read about modern China in preparation for the journey, I got a picture of a country careering down the path of market-driven development, like an overloaded truck that's just boiled its way over a mountain pass and is rocketing down the other side. This nation of a billion or more was posting double-digit growth year after year while the rest of the world watched and crossed its fingers that the brakes wouldn't fail. Reports of corruption, crime, even peasant riots, were emerging with greater and greater frequency. Years of high inflation had fed a growing restlessness that had culminated in the 1989 protests at Tiananmen Square. A heavy dose of the iron fist had dealt with that problem for the time being. But ultimately, I suppose, I wanted to discover if the communist regime in 1994 was at the beginning of its own period of dynastic decline, with all the implications that would have of dislocation and catastrophe.

Burma, on the other hand, was an area of darkness to me. All I knew about it was what I read in the papers and what I had learned from a few friends who'd visited on short-term tourist visas. The universal feeling seemed to be that it was a land in a time warp, ruled by a military dictatorship that was at once shockingly repressive and pitifully incompetent. The country had been in self-imposed isolation since the early 1960s. In contrast to China, Burma had actually gone backwards from being one of the richest countries in Asia to an economic basket case.

In January 1993 I began making serious plans. I contacted the *Sydney Morning Herald*, which expressed an interest in a series of articles from the journey, and I approached publishers. I consulted China experts and Burma experts. I met Morrison's surviving son, Alastair. I went to the Mitchell Library in Sydney and rummaged through Morrison's vast collection of diaries, notes, letters, photographs, maps and memorabilia. I reread *Morrison of Peking* and went through *An Australian in China* with a fine-tooth comb.

I dug up old maps of China and Burma and, by plotting the old place names that appeared in Morrison's book against the most up-to-date maps I could find, I soon had the entire route sketched out. Sometimes it followed the modern highway system, sometimes it meandered through the countryside. I decided not to walk the highways — dodging trucks and breathing diesel fumes seemed a little beside the point of the whole exercise — but, rather, to do what Morrison had set out to do. I would sail up the Yangtze, and then I would catch buses, hitchhike or walk, sleeping in truckstops and village inns, eating peasant food. I would travel and live as a local.

But before all this daydreaming could become reality, there was another problem to be solved: money. As usual, I had virtually none of it. So I put together a proposal and began mailing it out to some of the many Australian companies that are doing business in China. To my amazement and delight, several of them responded, and within a couple of months I had all the support I needed.

It had all come together so quickly that I found myself, sometime in the first half of 1993, with my plans so far advanced that I decided to leave ahead of schedule. To start from Shanghai on 11th February 1994, the exact anniversary of Morrison's departure, might have been in keeping with the spirit of the original, but it would have involved travelling in the depths of the Chinese winter. It would also have meant arriving in Burma during the monsoon. Rugged adventurers take such things in their stride, of course, but extremes of climate do present problems for photographers. So I decided to leave at the beginning of September, which would allow me to experience the Yangtze during the wonderful Chinese autumn, and arrive in Burma before the onset of the hot season, with its blinding light, useless for photography.

The only obstacle left was the small matter of the language. I hired a tutor, Tanya, and although I think I spent more time talking about the trip with her and her husband, Wei, than practising my vocabulary, after about three months I had enough Mandarin to survive in places where a foreigner mightn't have been seen in fifty years. I mangled the tones and botched the word order, but I was pretty confident that in an emergency I'd be able to ask directions to the bathroom and catch the reply before it was too late.

And then it was time to go.

中国

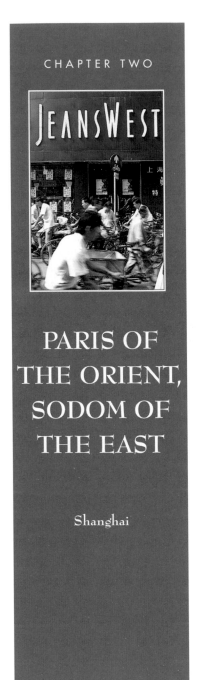

CHAPTER TWO

PARIS OF
THE ORIENT,
SODOM OF
THE EAST

Shanghai

I emerged from the dingy chambers of the hotel and took a look at Shanghai by day. The hotel, I noticed, seemed to be an island in the middle of an enormous construction site which threatened to swamp it at any moment. I don't know what stood here in Morrison's time, but I suspect it was a muddy field and a couple of overworked draught animals. Nowadays it is just another specimen of that scrappy, grey, half-finished concrete monotony that characterises most modern Chinese cities. I hailed a cab and took myself off somewhere more interesting.

Shanghai

Morrison wrote almost nothing about his visit to Shanghai, but this doesn't mean there was nothing to write about. Shanghai in 1894 was a kind of Wild West boomtown in the Far East, a metropolis of one million souls that, with the help of the trade of half of China, had mushroomed from an old walled town on a swampy riverbank in the space of just fifty years. It was a city of tycoons, drunken sailors, proselytising priests, merchants, refugees, gangsters, beggars and whores, of muddy lanes and palatial mansions, of hellish factories and glittering emporia. It was brash, cynical, ambitious, a place of incalculable wealth and unimaginable poverty, a Western enclave hemmed in by the Pacific Ocean on one side and the Chinese landmass on the other, protected by treaties and privileges that made it unique, a community free of obligation and responsibility, a community created for the sole purpose of the accumulation of wealth, by whatever means it might take. I wanted to see how much of that Shanghai had survived, and I had a fair idea where to start looking.

After half an hour battling bicycles, buses and exhaust fumes, I jumped out under the steel girders of Waibaidu Bridge, walked across and took a look at a sight which was already familiar from a dozen photos. In front of me was the murky yellow-brown of the Huangpu River, throbbing with freighters, ferries, tugs and launches. To one side a world-weary waterway known to Westerners as Suzhou Creek disgorged a continuous stream of chugging barges and stinking, oily black water. On a wide concrete walk that hugged the riverbank for a kilometre or so, septuagenarian men and women performed surprising feats of contortion in the name of tai chi. Middle-aged couples were taking ballroom dancing classes to plonky piano music, while younger ones strolled up and down in crisply ironed shirts and high heels.

Behind me, a line of imposing but very un-Oriental looking buildings bore down on the whole scene. They reminded me more than anything of those chunky bakelite radios from the thirties that trendy secondhand shops in Sydney are always trying to flog off at preposterous prices. An undulating rank of fine old valve radios, a bit dusty but otherwise quite serviceable — this was my first impression of Shanghai's famous Bund.

Once the centre of the International Settlement, the Bund was the headquarters of Western commerce in China. If you were looking for the point on earth where East meets West, or where they first got to know each other, or at least once had a passionate, anarchic, century-long, love–hate fling, this would have to be it. In Shanghai were born both Chinese capitalism and Chinese communism. The capitalists had loved it and the communists had spurned it. But reminders of its extraordinary past were everywhere to be seen.

The Bund, with its banks and consulates and five-star hotels was, for many foreigners, the first thing they saw as their ships nosed their way carefully up the narrow waters of the Huangpu to dock by the city. Enervated after their long voyages from San Francisco, London, Hong Kong or a dozen other places, the earnest missionaries, the diplomats, the financiers, the penniless clerks, the fortune hunters, the con-men, the tourists, the journalists and the adventurers would clatter across the gangplank, wobble for a moment on dry land and see — what? What would Morrison have seen when his ship pulled in here from Tokyo in the first week of February 1894?

The closest equivalent in the modern world of the old Shanghai is, of course, Hong Kong. Both were wrenched from China at the point of a gun in 1842 in the First Opium War. Both are ports built largely by foreign powers to help them tap the vast wealth of China. One has already reverted to China, the other soon will. Anyone who has stood by the Star Ferry terminal at Kowloon and looked across to the glass towers of Hong Kong island would have some idea of what the Bund and its tidy array of counting houses would have meant to the visitor in 1894.

Most of the architecture on the Bund dates from the early decades of the twentieth century. But it only replaced earlier versions of the same thing. I have seen photos of Shanghai from the 1890s, and if what greeted me on the Bund that day was worthy early twentieth-century colonial stodge, then what greeted Morrison 100 years before had simply been worthy late nineteenth-century colonial stodge.

What else would he have seen? The river would have been alive with everything from sleek steamers to creaking sailboats, with perhaps a foreign gunboat or two as a subtle reminder to the locals. Each ship, as soon as it arrived, was besieged by a swarm of junks, sampans and lighters. Some would take the cargo — everything from shining machinery to sticky opium — to the burgeoning warehouses and factories that were fast absorbing the fields and villages around the city. Others served a different purpose: unloading kitchen scraps for distribution to Shanghai's thousands of beggars. Plying the river would have been bamboo rafts loaded with farm produce, fishing junks and reeking nightsoil barges.

Looking across the river in 1993, the dominant feature was the half-finished Shanghai telecommunications tower, piercing the sky like a vast concrete rocket preparing for takeoff.

Lining the Bund in either direction would have been a forest of masts, belonging to the hundreds of small boats more or less permanently moored to the bank. In the boats, children would have jumped surefooted from plank to plank, women sang and sewed rags while their husbands, the coolies, swarmed across the Bund loading and unloading cargo, chanting as they worked, much to the irritation of the mutton-chopped merchants poring over their balance-sheets in the granite edifices opposite. Along the thoroughfare, now known as Zhongshan Road East, would have been rickshaws, wheelbarrows, handcarts and horsecarts, all drawn by sweating scrawny beasts of burden, be they animal or human.

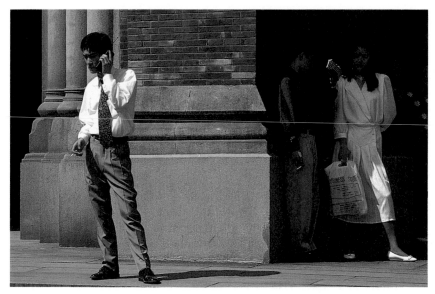

TOP AND BOTTOM: *St Ignatius Cathedral, Xujiahui, Shanghai*

Shanghai's Bund. At centre is the Customs House, with the former Hongkong & Shanghai Bank at centre left, and the former Shanghai Club at far left

Nanjing Road, Shanghai

Street scene in Wuhan

Along much of the bank ran the Public Gardens, whose lush lawns, rose beds and bandstand had been created by a British gardener brought out for this specific purpose. At the entrance to this park stood a notice forbidding Chinese to enter. The site has been renamed Huangpu Park and, like many a modern Chinese park, now consists of a large expanse of concrete dotted with a few flower beds. But for the people who gather there to chat, play and stroll, it's a precious bit of open space in a manicly claustrophobic city.

Crossing Zhongshan Road, its wheelbarrows and rickshaws long since replaced by taxis and trucks and buses jammed with bodies, I took a closer look at the architecture. Two buildings dominate the Bund. One was once the headquarters of the Imperial Maritime Customs, which in Morrison's time was operated by an international staff employed by the Chinese. The building was now just a grimy cube of sulphurous yellow, but the obelisk of its clock tower, thrusting high above its neighbours, testified to its authority.

Next door, not as tall as the Customs House but twice as wide, looking like a well-fed financier in a comfy armchair, sat what was once the joint head office of the Hongkong & Shanghai Bank, a squat Winston Churchill of a building crowned with a whitish dome like a bald pate. Founded in 1864, the bank had been the largest foreign financial institution in China, the spearhead of Western colonial penetration. This particular building was put up in the 1920s. Now, on either side of the dome, two poles flew the red flag of the People's Republic. From where I stood, they looked like little markers on some Cold War campaign map, sprouting incongruously from Winnie's temples.

When the communists took over in 1949, the bank's office was told to move into much humbler premises and the building became the new office of the Shanghai Municipal Government. Vengeance must have been sweet.

In 1994 the administration can no longer justify the cost of occupying such a valuable piece of real estate. So the lease on the building has been put out to tender. Among those considering making a bid is the Hongkong & Shanghai Bank, which is now back in China doing business. Refurbishing the building after nearly fifty years of neglect will be expensive but, as this book goes to press, they're considering it.

A little further up the road stood what had once been the Shanghai Club (now the Dongfeng Hotel), built by the British in 1910 as an exclusive retreat for the upper echelons of the foreign community. It boasted a library, reading room, billiard rooms and, reputedly, the longest bar in the world at which industrialists, Yangtze riverboat captains and young executives drank in strict pecking order. Looking at it from the outside, I could almost picture the leather armchairs and the starched white tablecloths.

When I took a look inside I could see that it still had a bar, but it was now furnished with black vinyl seats and was deserted. Downstairs, at street level, things were busier. It was a Kentucky Fried Chicken outlet. I turned into Nanjing Road which meets the Bund at right angles. Now — as in 1894 — it is the greatest shopping thoroughfare in Shanghai, perhaps in China.

Nanjing Road had changed, no doubt, but its flavour was much as I had imagined it. In Morrison's day it was lined with silk shops, sweet shops, music shops, fur shops, sports shops, jewellery shops, jade shops, coffin shops, pawn shops and hardware shops, each advertising their wares with a vertical sign in gold and black. The traffic was directed by huge Sikh policemen in red turbans, brought across from India by the British.

Nowadays there are shops full of Shiseido perfume and Playboy clothes, and a giant sign in neon advertises White Rabbit sweets. At the turn of the century those with money in Shanghai could get anything from California grapefruit to Cadbury's chocolate to a Steinway piano. In 1994, for the first time since 1949, Rolls-Royce showrooms opened in Beijing, Guangdong and Shanghai.

It was time for lunch. I entered a little hole-in-the-wall restaurant and sat down. A woman in a grubby white apron came over, beaming from ear to ear, gushed forth a stream of good-natured but incomprehensible Chinese and handed me a menu. I suppose I shouldn't have been, but when I opened it I was vaguely surprised to discover that it, too, was in Chinese.

The moment had arrived. I couldn't put off testing my precarious command of the language any longer. Shutting the menu I said, as carefully as I could, '*Mantou?*' This, I remembered, meant steamed bun, which I'd already seen for sale in the streets. The waitress nodded and stood there. I realised that she expected me to ask for something else. So I said the only other thing I could think of: '*Shu cai*' — 'vegetables'.

Twenty minutes later, the mantou arrived. It looked as though the cook had taken some of those polystyrene pellets they pack electronic equipment in, and microwaved them till they swelled to the size of eggs. I tried one. It tasted like I'd always imagined a microwaved polystyrene pellet to taste. Another ten minutes and the vegetable arrived. It was some distant relative of spinach, stir-fried and dripping with soy. So this is how it's going to be, I thought. Well, at least the soy covered the taste of polystyrene.

Outside, a little old man with a wispy beard and a cap with fur-lined flaps turned up above his ears was tending a clay stove. A pile of hot, freshly baked flatbreads lay by his side, 5 *mao* (half a yuan, or 10 Australian cents) apiece. I had some the next day. Inside the golden-brown, crusty dough, a sprinkle of sugar had just turned liquid with the heat. They were wonderful.

* * *

Shanghai's foreign concessions thrived until World War II, when the Japanese took over. During their heyday in the 1920s and 1930s, they were a magnet for refugees fleeing war and starvation, gangsters fleeing justice and revolutionaries seeking asylum. Many of these people ended up in the French Concession, where the police had a reputation for, shall we say, flexibility. One such fugitive was Du Yuesheng who, as head of the Green Gang, dominated the city's multi-million-dollar opium trade. Another was Zhou Enlai.

I was wandering about amid the plane trees and the stucco houses with their shuttered windows, hoping vaguely to come across a café selling croissants. There was no such thing, of course. Any such city in the West would have trumpeted its French past to every passing tourist with a dollar to spend, but here the locals just swished hurriedly by on their big black bikes, intent on a Chinese future, not a foreign past. It was like Quebec in reverse, and it was refreshing.

'Where you from?' said a voice behind me. He was young, in ironed pants and a white shirt.

'Australia.'

He looked puzzled. I tried again.

'*Aodaliya.*'

'Oh, Aodaliya. Aodaliya is a very beautiful country. Which city?'

'*Xini,*' I gave the local pronunciation.

'Oh, Xini is a very beautiful city.'

'Um, how do you know?'

'Oh, I see Xini many times on TV. You very lucky.'

'Lucky? Why?'

'Why? Because Xini have the 2000 O-lym-pica. Not Beijing!'

I'd completely forgotten about the Olympics. The announcement of who had won the bid to stage the 2000 Games had been scheduled for the previous night, in the small hours of the morning. I'd thought about sitting up to watch, but fatigue had got the better of me.

'Are you sorry it didn't go to Beijing?' I asked him.

'For my national pride, I am sorry. But I think China cannot afford this thing. Now we have so many problems — already we spend so much money on sport. I think China only want this for political reason — so Li Peng [Premier] can say, look how big country China is, we can do this thing. I think it is better it go to Xini.'

'I think many people in Australia want it for political reasons, too.'

He looked puzzled again. 'But I thought Aodaliya is democracy?'

'Yes. And now people will use the Olympics to try and win the next election.' Light dawned in his eyes, and he smiled.

'I want to study in Aodaliya,' he told me, and gave me his card, which was thin and papery. His name was Wu, and he had a diploma in commerce.

'Perhaps you can help me. China is no good just now. China is a capitalist country, only it keep calling itself communist. I want to study computer science.'

There wasn't much I could do to help him, but this was difficult to explain.

Later I heard reports of people crying on the streets of Beijing when the announcement was made about the Olympics. But in Shanghai, if I hadn't run into Wu, I probably wouldn't even have realised it had happened. I got the impression the people of Shanghai didn't pay much attention to what went on in Beijing.

I wandered on, got lost, found my way again, and eventually got to my destination. It was a two-storey, dark brick building standing on a corner, with elegant double doors and shuttered windows painted red. Somehow it didn't look quite right — a little too perfect, if anything. I went up close and discovered the reason. The exterior was not brick at all, but a kind of custom-made brick veneer that matched the house with those around it.

I was looking at the place where the Chinese Communist Party had been founded by thirteen delegates, including Mao Zedong, in 1921. Inside, it was immaculately tidy, and deserted. One room had been redecorated exactly as it had been for the founding conference, including table and teacups. I tried hard to picture the scene, to feel the passion and the vision and the anger of those far-off people. But all I could think was that the place looked as if it had been rebuilt from the ground up some time since 1949.

Black and white photos, blurred and grainy, lined the walls in the other rooms, and there were displays of capitalist repression from the bad old days: a clock that had been used to time mill workers' actions, a truncheon to crack strikers over the head. Amid the memorabilia was a group photo of Chinese communists taken in Paris in 1924. In the front row, his face turned to an empty white oval by the thousands of fingers that had sought him out, sat Zhou Enlai. At the rear stood another figure whose features were also almost worn off: a boyish Deng Xiaoping. Jesus, I thought, this guy is seriously *old*. He was a card-carrying communist when Ronald Reagan was still running around with a toy gun pretending to be Tom Mix.

By 1927 the gangster Du Yuesheng had become so powerful that when the communists rose to take Shanghai, Chiang Kai-shek, the head of the Guomindang government, called him in to eject them. The Green Gang took to the streets with the ferocity of professional hoodlums and in a matter of days Shanghai's communists lay dead in their thousands. The Party abandoned the idea of taking the urban areas and retreated to the countryside to launch the peasant revolution that would deliver them power twenty-two years later. When they marched back into Shanghai in 1949, they did it virtually without firing a shot. But Mao would never forget Chiang's betrayal.

For more than a century until 1949 men like Deng watched while the colonial powers in their worst moments took control of their largest ports, established enclaves from which the Chinese were excluded, repeatedly humiliated their government at the point of a gun, flooded the country with narcotics, demanded and got access to every corner of the country, and armed and manipulated corrupt, cruel and ineffectual regimes for the sake of preserving their lucrative trade. If Deng is capable of a coherent thought today, I imagine he looks with indulgence from his ninety years at the downy-cheeked lads who seem to be perpetually failing their driving tests at the steering wheels of Western democracies. Billy and Johnny may get the odd sweetie tossed to them by the great-grandfathers in Beijing, but that's as far as it will go.

I was wandering back down the street, having forgotten the old communist museum as quickly as any kid on a school excursion, when a figure darted out in front of me. He was in his twenties, in jeans and a Lacoste T-shirt. A mobile phone was hitched to his waist.

'Please come and see my nightclub!' he implored in English.

I looked behind him. He was gesturing at a marble facade that housed an elaborate entrance arch. Set into the wall on either side of the door, 3 metres (10 feet) high apiece, were two wonderful sculptures of voluptuous bare-breasted women in loin cloths, their arms opened in an embrace that made them look like a combination of *Penthouse* Pet and Christ on the cross.

'It is called the Rome Club. It will open next month. Please come and look,' insisted my new friend.

I followed him inside. The air was choked with sawdust and the shrieking of power tools, but the shape of the nightclub-to-be was very much there. Wei, the manager, pointed out the dance floor, with its state-of-the-art sound system and impressive bank of lights, and the richly decorated bar. 'There are twelve private rooms,' he went on, 'each to be decorated in a different national style — British, Japanese, American and so on.'

'Are there many nightclubs in Shanghai?' I asked.

'Until last year they were not permitted. Now there are about twenty. But this will be the best. Please come when it opens, and bring all your friends. Entry will cost 100 yuan.'

I didn't have the heart to tell him that in a month's time the company executive he obviously took me for would probably be footslogging it around the mountains of eastern Sichuan where 100 yuan will last a week. I doubt he'd have understood why, and I couldn't blame him.

* * *

But I was still in Shanghai, and that night I went to JJ's. Chinese pop music was jangling over the speakers as I handed over my money to the mini-skirted, lip-glossed hostess at Shanghai's biggest disco.

The club was a big black space with two dance floors, a gallery, video screens and a big pit with room for half a dozen DJs; the decor was an amalgam of the styles of the seventies, eighties and nineties, in no particular order. The smaller dance floor was already crowded with boppers, Chinese and Western. On the stage at the front, a floor show was in action. Half a dozen girls in hot pants were doing a choreographed number as mist from a smoke machine rose from the floor. Their T-shirts carried the Tampax logo. I took up a spot by the bar. Around me were Chinese in lounge suits, Chinese in black jeans, black skivvies and dark glasses, Chinese in baseball caps and 501s.

Suddenly the place darkened, the music cut out and the floor show ended. The theme from *Star Wars* began to play, deafeningly loudly. Above my head, a heavy lighting installation, presumably meant to resemble a spaceship, started to move across the ceiling. People started to cheer and whistle. Five minutes later it had reached its destination in the middle of the room. The *Star Wars* music ended and a rap song from America started up. The banks of video monitors burst with colour, the smoke machines belched and the dance floor exploded into movement.

A voice shouted in my ear. 'My name is Lily,' it said. 'Are you from America?'

'No,' I yelled back. 'Are you from Shanghai?'

'No,' she said, naming a town in the hinterland unknown to me. It occurred to me to ask her what she did for a living, but then I thought better of it.

'Do you want to dance with me?' she asked. 'It will cost 20 *kuai* [yuan]. Or you can come and dance at my flat.'

'At your flat?'

'That will cost 500.'

'I don't think so.'

Later I saw her leave on the arm of a prosperous looking Chinese man. By two in the morning, JJ's was dying, and I left for the long trek back to my hotel.

In 1866 an estimated one in twelve of the Chinese households in and around Shanghai was a brothel. The most common diseases among foreign residents were gonorrhoea and syphilis. There were prostitutes of every class, catering to every purse. In the 1930s the city was bursting with nightclubs, as a guidebook from the period attests (see opposite).

The same book a few pages later notes blandly that in 1933 some 5,715 'exposed corpses' were collected in the city — beggars, unwanted infants, victims of cold, starvation and disease. The municipality had trucks and workers specifically employed to collect the bodies from the footpaths each morning.

'If God lets Shanghai endure, He owes an apology to Sodom and Gomorrah,' wrote the American evangelist Harry Franck in 1925. God might work in mysterious ways, but Mao had ideas of his own. In 1949 the communists marched

Whoopee!

What odds whether Shanghai is the Paris of the East or Paris the Shanghai of the Occident?

Dog races and cabarets, hai-alai and cabarets, formal tea and dinner dances and cabarets, the sophisticated and cosmopolitan French Club and cabarets, the dignified and formal Country Club and cabarets, prize fights and cabarets, amateur dramatics and cabarets, theatres and cabarets, movies and cabarets, and cabarets — everywhere, in both extremities of Frenchtown, uptown and downtown in the International Settlement, in Hongkew, and out of bounds in Chinese territory, are cabarets.

Hundreds of 'em!
High hats and low necks; long tails and short knickers; inebriates and slumming puritans.
Wine, women and song.

Whoopee!

Let's go places and do things!
When the sun goes in and the lights come out Shanghai becomes another city, the City of Blazing Night, a night life Haroun-al-Raschid never knew, with tales Scheherezade never told the uxoricidal Sultan Shahriyar...
The throb of the jungle tom-tom; the symphony of lust; the music of a hundred orchestras; the shuffling of feet; the swaying of bodies; the rhythm of abandon; the hot smoke of desire — desire under the floodlights; it's all fun; it's life.

Joy, gin, and jazz. There's nothing puritanical about Shanghai.

into the city, Du Yuesheng fled to Hong Kong with the remnants of his Green Gang, and the good old days came to a very sudden end.

* * *

One Sunday morning I endured a gut-crunching ride on a motorcycle taxi to St Ignatius Cathedral at Xujiahui, at the edge of the city. For over an hour I sat rigid, clinging for dear life to tripod and camera bag, suffering the stiff suspension on the half-made roads as we passed a great wall of half-finished high-rise housing estates, an endless loop of urban anonymity. When we arrived there, it seemed almost unbelievable: a red-brick, double-spired cathedral, rose window and all, rising above the desert of cement. It had once been the centrepiece of a Jesuit mission that included factories, schools and a sophisticated observatory.

The morning's service was over and it was almost unnervingly peaceful inside the big, cool, grey chamber of the nave. In the middle, a clutch of a dozen or so ancient worshippers, men and women, were kneeling among the dark pews fingering their rosaries, praying with a sound that was more like a Buddhist chant. In that space they seemed withered and small, far-off and oblivious, marooned on this silent island. Waiting for release, perhaps.

I took some pictures and stepped outside. Guests were beginning to arrive for a wedding: a man from Ohio was marrying a local. I was just tossing up whether to try and insinuate myself into this friendly crowd or join battle once more with the traffic when a Chinese man appeared with a tripod and a couple of cameras. I assumed he was the wedding photographer until he opened his mouth.

'Pretty good church, eh?' he said.

'Pretty good,' I agreed.

'It was built in 1910. You see the steeples?'

'Yes.' It was hard not to.

'Both of those were knocked down during the Cultural Revolution. Completely destroyed. Then in the eighties, they built them right back up again. Amazing.'

I tried to picture it, and it was a shocking image, this thought of the church minus its steeples. It was tempting to write it off as meaningless, a mindless act of destruction, yet its meaning was all too clear. We all know the urge to deface, the kind of anger that vents itself on buildings that are at once powerful and defenceless. What got me was the restitution — how, fifteen or twenty years later, people had come back and calmly rebuilt it so that now it looked as if nothing had ever happened. That was the bit I couldn't quite fathom.

'My name is Jim,' he was telling me. 'I am a tour guide with China International Travel Service. My hobby is to photograph old buildings. Here is my card. Perhaps you would like to visit me some time.'

A couple of mornings later I went to see Jim at his flat. He lived there with his mother, his wife and their children. They had two whole floors to themselves.

'You're lucky to have a space like this in Shanghai,' I commented.

'Yes,' he agreed. 'My family has been here a long time, so we are better off than most. For most people in Shanghai it is difficult even to find a place to rent. But look at this.'

He had produced a stack of photo albums, fifteen or more of them. 'My father was a businessman before the Revolution. In his spare time he used to take a lot of photos. Now it is my hobby to find the same places and photograph them as they are now. Actually, I inherited this place from my father. During the Cultural Revolution he was criticised as a counter-revolutionary and Red Guards invaded the house. They burned or destroyed many of his papers, but fortunately most of the photos survived. I was just a boy, but I remember it well.'

I started to flip through the albums. What I saw surprised me, not because of how much had changed but rather, how little. Department stores had become offices, cinemas had become public halls, churches had become factories. But the original buildings were still recognisable. To look at it all properly would have taken a day.

'Have you thought about publishing a book?' I asked after a while.

'Of course,' he said. 'I even had a publisher interested. But the authorities were not in favour. It does not look good for them. They are ashamed that Shanghai has developed so little!'

When the communists took over, they decided to teach Shanghai a lesson, to bring the wild, radical city to heel once and for all, and at the same time spread industrial development more evenly throughout China. For decades, the wealth generated by Shanghai was siphoned off to fund the development of other areas while the city was left to moulder. In the first Five Year Plan, a staggering sixty-four per cent of the capital for all basic construction investment for industry *for the whole of China* came out of Shanghai.

'But now many of these buildings are disappearing,' said Jim. 'Many foreign businesses are coming to Shanghai now. Land in the city is valuable, and they have to make way for new offices and expensive apartments.'

In a city crammed with ironies, this had to be the greatest irony of them all. The spirit of the old Shanghai, tough and fast, is as strong as ever. But the city itself, this extraordinary relic, which has survived war, revolution and neglect, is being destroyed by the return of the very capitalism that built it.

CHAPTER THREE

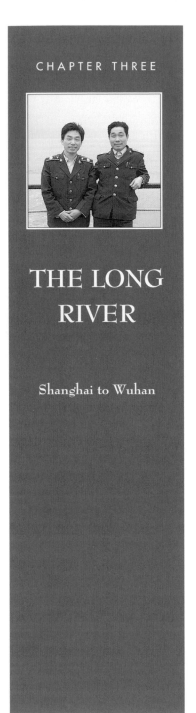

THE LONG RIVER

Shanghai to Wuhan

The big passenger boat slipped quietly from the dock and into the Huangpu River. The day's heavy rain had eased to a light drizzle, and the purplish hue of dusk hung over the city. Behind my head, a crackly loudspeaker was playing a mangled version of 'Jingle Bells' with a disco beat.

On a boat on the Yangtze River

I stood by the rail as we slid past the Bund. The Customs House clock tower chimed a quarter to seven. These bells, cast in Britain and installed in the 1920s, were reportedly reconfigured to play 'The East is Red' during the reign of Mao Zedong. Now, once again, they toll the Westminster chimes. I caught a brief, final glimpse of flashing neon as we drew abreast of Nanjing Road, and then the black industrial chaos of the shoreline turned steadily blacker as the last of the day disappeared. I was on my way into the real China, whatever that might turn out to be.

The other passengers had already withdrawn to the cabins and were engrossed in mah-jong, cards, cigarettes and instant noodles. In my cabin people were washing shirts or trousers in the tiny basin in the corner of the room, or lying on their bunks staring into space. I got out my book and had a read.

By next morning the city had disappeared, its place taken by an infinity of opaque water. The sun was shining brightly on the dull river and people were spitting and drinking tea from jam jars, the big leaves swimming in the murky green liquid. I never did figure out how to drink it without getting a mouthful of tea leaves.

The river looked more like a lake — wide, flat and empty. When Marco Polo reported that in its lower reaches the Yangtze runs 16 kilometres (10 miles) wide in the rainy season, the folks back in Venice thought he was having them on. But he wasn't. The shore on either side was a narrow, flat, greenish-brown line far off in the distance. If there was any human presence there at all, it couldn't be discerned from where I sat. And this when the high water of summer had been and gone.

The occasional grimy barge or passenger boat identical to ours chugged past. The water was a brown silty sludge, a similar colour to the stuff I was now drinking from a huge white and blue enamel mug: Nescafe with Coffee-Mate, which in most parts of China is the only alternative to the ubiquitous green tea. I suspect a cup of Yangtze water would have tasted pretty similar, too.

Morrison left Shanghai on the river steamer *Taiwo*, no doubt with the sound of firecrackers ringing in his ears. He had a cabin to himself, and paid the steward to bring him 'foreign chow'. To the delight of his Scots soul, his Chinese outfit got him a $2 discount from a chief officer, who took him for a missionary. And that's all he tells us about the steamer from Shanghai to Wuhan, a service that had already been operating for over thirty years. It was 11th February 1894. A thousand kilometres (600 miles) away in Hunan Province, a six-week old baby called Mao Zedong was screaming for attention.

I was sharing a cabin with nine others, and one look at the boat's kitchen banished all thoughts of 'chow', foreign or otherwise, immediately from my mind. There were four classes of accommodation: deck, which was no more or less than exactly that, wherever you could find space to spread a blanket; fourth, which was twenty or more berths to a cabin and where passengers spat and threw rubbish on the floor with a cheerful abandon; third, where I was, with ten bunks to a room and where gobbing was frowned on; and second, two berths to a cabin, where you could presumably get up to anything you liked. There was no first class since China is a socialist country.

My outfit, at least, was pretty close to a Chinese outfit — or rather, most Chinese people these days wear Western clothes — jeans and sneakers and T-shirts. The Mao suit — blue, grey or, most commonly, green — is still popular in the countryside, but in the cities it has gone the way of the *Little Red Book*. Maybe it will come back in one of these days, along with the Mao badges and red stars that I had seen on trendy Shanghai teenagers. But if I'd really wanted to imitate the style of the nineties' Chinese urban male, as displayed by everyone from rickshaw peddlers to office workers, I'd have been in shiny shoes, a white shirt with a collar, and a double-breasted suit bought from a street stall for around A$10.

Unfortunately, the cuffs of these suits usually came to somewhere just below my knees, so jeans and a T-shirt it was. Maybe it was the lack of an ill-fitting suit, but nobody took *me* for a missionary.

As for women, everyone — *everyone*, from Shanghai hairdressers to the peasant woman planting rice with a baby on her back — was in acrylic ski pants, brown or black. This was usually accompanied by high heels and a colourful sweater or a jacket, also of some kind of acrylic. The most popular hairstyle consists of having the hair at the sides and back crimped and tied back in a pony tail, while the top is teased into a quiff that would have done Elvis proud.

One of my cabin-mates offered me a cigarette. This is the universal gesture of friendship among Chinese males. Something like — well, I guess we don't really have a universal gesture of friendship in the West, do we?

'*Bu yao*,' I responded — 'I don't.' He looked a little taken aback, and proceeded to light up, along with every other man in the room. None of the women smoked, I noticed. They didn't need to — just breathing in was enough.

'What is your country name?' the man asked.

'Aodaliya.'

'Oh. Aodaliya is a very beautiful country,' he said.

'I know,' I responded, anxious to short-circuit a conversation I'd already had half a dozen times. 'Where do you come from?'

'We come from Wuhan,' he said, and everyone else in the cabin nodded affirmation.

This seemed to be about the limit of his English, and of everyone else's. Then a young woman took over. She was in high heels, ski pants, an acrylic sweater and a jacket. Her hair was in a stylish bob, and her name was Rong Li.

'I am going to Wuhan,' I said slowly. 'What is Wuhan like?'

'Wuhan is a very beautiful city,' said Rong Li in the delightful singsong with which Chinese women speak English. I don't know why, but I had a sneaking suspicion that this opinion might bear more relation to a high-school English textbook than to any real consideration of urban aesthetics. I know a lot of people who've been to China, but I'd never met anyone who'd visited Wuhan. All I knew about it was that it had a lot of heavy industry.

'How do you like Shanghai?' I asked.

'It is very crowded,' said Rong Li. 'We work for a clothing company. We went there for a — *zenme shuo?* [how do you say?] — trade fair. Now we are going home. I will be happy to get home. In Shanghai I spent too much money!'

'What is your job?' I asked her.

'I am manager's secretary.'

'Do you like doing that?'

'It is so-so. I want to be in marketing. I studied it in college. But now I am young. Maybe I will get a chance in future.'

'Did you learn English at college, too?'

'Yes. This is part of my work now, to translate documents for my company. Now we do a lot of business with foreign companies, and I am the only person in the company who can speak English. Everybody learns English for six years at school, but most people never learn to speak it properly. All they can say is "hello" and "goodbye". So many companies will give me a job. Actually, this is the first time I have spoken English to a — how do you say? — native. It is funny for me!'

I asked her how old she was. She was twenty-two. It was her first trip out of Wuhan. She was still living with her parents.

'Would you like to work in Shanghai one day?'

'No, never! Everybody want to work in Shanghai. But I like Wuhan.'

The boys were playing some kind of eternal card game, and we joined in for a while. I was given sweets and mandarins. More cigarettes were handed round. I was the only foreigner on the boat.

* * *

That day passed, and another one. Sometimes we would pull into shore, to murky cities, and tie up for an hour or so at ugly docks of oily steel, while passengers shuffled on and off, weighed down by big cloth bags of I don't know what. One of these places must have been Nanjing, sometime capital of China, but I couldn't tell it from the rest. Then we would set sail again, the riverbanks once more distant, deserted.

On the last afternoon one of the cabin attendants, a jovial middle-aged woman, came around selling tickets, red slips of paper, for 2 kuai (yuan) each. With a big grin she gave me two for free. I was honoured, but mystified.

'Today is China's national day,' explained Rong Li. 'It is also the autumn festival. There will be a party.'

Now I understood. It was the first of October, the anniversary of the day Mao stood at the top of Tiananmen Square in 1949 and proclaimed the founding of the People's Republic. As it was full moon, it was also the culmination of the mid-autumn festival, where families traditionally get together and give each other moon cakes — heavy pastries full of fruit mince. Little stalls were selling them everywhere and I had been stuffing myself with them for the last week, oblivious to their significance.

Everyone spent about an hour getting ready. The men took out crisp white shirts and suits which, through some mysterious and semi-miraculous process, they had managed to keep neatly pressed. The women put on make-up and miniskirts. I felt like a mug in my jeans and mountain boots, much as I had at JJ's. At seven-thirty sharp we all marched down to the deck below to start the festivities, picking our way over the dozing bodies in deck class.

The ship's ballroom was about 10 metres by 3 (30 feet by 10), with a lino floor and plastic chandeliers. Seats were arranged around the edges and multicoloured fairy lights were draped from the ceiling. Behind a table, two men were fiddling with a tape player. There were no drinks and no food. We sat down on the chairs and waited for the music to start.

When it did, it was a tape of a small orchestra with wailing strings. Everyone leaped to their feet. The numbers were a succession of foxtrots, tangos, cha-chas, rumbas — all those ballroom dances which I'd vaguely assumed developed in about the 1920s and disappeared sometime around the fifties, and which I've never really been able to distinguish from each other. The Chinese had all the steps down pat.

'Why don't you dance?' asked Rong Li.

'I only know disco,' I replied feebly. 'How do you know all these dances?'

'We learn them in school. Come, I will teach you.'

She made a valiant attempt, but she wasn't any more successful than anyone else who's ever tried to teach me to cha-cha. We made a few ungainly sweeps round the floor, then sat down to talk again.

In the meantime I'd noticed something else. Two uniformed soldiers were dancing together. They were both men. A little later, two women took to the floor together.

It wasn't long before the inevitable happened. A young man came over. 'Hello,' he said. 'My name is Wang. I am a law student from Wuhan. Would you care to dance with me?'

I got up and took his hand. 'Sorry,' I said. 'I dance very badly.'

'No,' he said politely. 'You dance very well.'

Then his girlfriend came and did a turn. As soon as the song finished, she fled, giggling, to her friends.

Finally some music came on that I recognised, and for a moment I was back at a school social in Canberra in flared cords and a check shirt. The band was Boney M. I grabbed Rong Li and we hit the floor; everyone else had fled from the thudding beat. A couple more numbers, and the party was over. The music stopped and the lights came on. We all went back to our cabins. It was nine-thirty exactly. The next morning we arrived at Wuhan.

I looked at my map and realised I had already crossed a fair slice of China. Over the last days, as I had read, talked, played cards, dozed off, waltzed, drunk tea and forced down plates of greasy bean curd and cold rice in the dining room, we had crossed three provinces. The homes of tens of millions had slipped by unseen. I was 1,000 kilometres (600 miles) inland, and my journey had barely even begun.

* * *

Wuhan was like Shanghai but slower, smaller: it had a population of five million, as compared to fifteen. Another row of French, British and Russian stone boxes faced the river. Another Opium War, another treaty, and in 1861 the Western powers had themselves another base, this time at China's most important inland port. Four rivers converge here or near by; for millennia, Wuhan has acted as the funnel for the vast wealth of the Yangtze valley.

Wuhan, Morrison wrote, 'is the mart of eight provinces and the centre of the earth. It is the chief distributing centre of the Yangtse valley, the capital city of the centre of China.' It has been sacked countless times; in the nineteenth century it changed hands four times during the Taiping Rebellion alone; it was taken briefly by the communists in 1927, and the Japanese in 1938. And every time it has bounced back, more vigorous than ever.

I could see at a glance that it was not, after all, a beautiful city.

I wandered around the remains of the foreign concession. At one end was the Customs House, as bold and imposing as its counterpart in Shanghai. But the rest of it — the British Consulate, the Banque de l'Indochine, the old residences — had been converted into offices or overcrowded apartments with washing hanging from the windows, giving only the faintest whiff of those long-gone days. In the alleyways in between, like the rising waters of a Yangtze flood, a market had taken over.

There were steamed buns, pancakes and fried dough sticks; tripe, pork, poultry, cabbages, pickled vegetables and leathery tofu swimming in a dubious watery brown sauce; dried fish and dead ducks; brooms, buckets, locks, taps, nails and rat traps. One lane was set aside for live produce: snakes, tortoises, frogs, catfish, silky hens and tiny kittens in cages. In one corner a row of men were squatting as they sliced up live eels. Each would take a wriggling eel from a bucket, impale it behind the head on a nail protruding from a board in front of him, and slit the creature lengthwise into four as it squirmed. The ground was sticky with blood, the stench sickening. The laneway was a constant war of attrition between stallholders, pedestrians, porters balancing bamboo poles over their shoulders and bicycle carts loaded with everything from mirrored wardrobes to half-finished plastic dolls. I battled my way through as the crowd thickened and thickened, until I was almost immobilised in a sweating sea of flesh. Slowly I worked my way on, past food stalls and fruit stalls and street-side acupuncturists and barbers shaving old men's heads with cut-throat razors, finally popping out on to a wide boulevard in the new part of town. It was heavy with smog, but it still felt like coming up for air. In front of me, a big billboard read 'COMPETITION AND ADVANCEMENT'.

* * *

That night I went out to dance with Rong Li; the place we went to was like the disco on the boat, only bigger and more expensive. The night started with a number from a band that was about eighty per cent crashing drums and twenty per cent Hammond organ. Then it was back to the ballroom stuff. I drank American Pabst beer, locally brewed, and she drank Coke.

'What does your father think of you coming out with a foreigner?' I asked her.

'He wouldn't like it. So I didn't tell him. He wants me to get married.'

'What does he do?'

'He is a teacher. So is my mother.'

'And your sister?'

'She is a teacher too.'

'Is she married?'

'Yes. Now she lives in a flat with her husband's parents.'

'Don't you want a flat of your own?'

'That is not possible,' she said with an air of finality. 'Even if I get married, it is difficult to find a flat.'

I was trying not to step on her feet during a rumba or a samba or a tango when a young man in a suit came over and said something unintelligible to me. He motioned to me to join his table, where seven or eight others were sitting. I thought he was just being friendly, but Rong Li wasn't interested.

'What did he want?' I asked when we sat down again.

'He wanted to change money,' she said.

We left at ten and I saw her on to her bus. It would take her an hour to get home. Back at the hotel, I collapsed into bed, exhausted.

* * *

中国

Wuhan, like Shanghai, had been visited by numerous Westerners by the time Morrison got there, so he doesn't spend much time describing either city. In Wuhan he mentions a modern cotton mill, a mint and an ironworks — unusual examples of industry at a time when China's rulers were mainly interested in the technology of modern weaponry so they could chuck out the barbarians and get back to being the Middle Kingdom.

Wuhan was the starting point for the 1911 rising that would finally finish off the doddering Qing dynasty. It was also the presence of an industrial working class that would make Wuhan, in 1927, the place where an angry mob, in an early communist rising, forced the British for the first time to lower the Union Jack from their consulate, presaging the end of the foreign concessions all over China within the next twenty years.

The Hanyang Ironworks is gone, bombed during the Sino-Japanese War; it has been replaced by the Wuhan Iron and Steel Complex, outside the city, which went into service in 1959. It now produces about twelve million tonnes of iron and steel a year, the second biggest output in China. On the old site now stands a textile mill, built since 1949. In 1895 cotton yarn and piece goods were the biggest items of import, surpassing even opium. European merchants confidently predicted that domestically produced cotton would never meet the standard of the foreign product. In 1994 I have a wardrobe full of cotton pants and shirts, most of which were made in China. China is the largest exporter of cotton cloth in the world, and a significant producer of textile machinery.

Before leaving Wuhan, I went to say goodbye to Rong Li at the office of her clothing company, which was upstairs in the decaying hulk of a former foreign godown. She was back in her power suit, every inch the manager's secretary. Her office was a renovated nightmare of chrome, white formica and glaring fluoro. I had a headache within five minutes.

'I think I will leave this job soon,' she said when we were alone. 'It is boring, and the pay is not enough — only 200 yuan per week.' Plenty of Chinese get about that much a month.

We had a glass of tea and she walked with me across to the boat terminal. I waved to her from the deck as the boat slid out into the river, the sunset sky a crimson gash across the horizon of cranes, docks and smokestacks. I bet she's got the job she wants by now. I wish her luck.

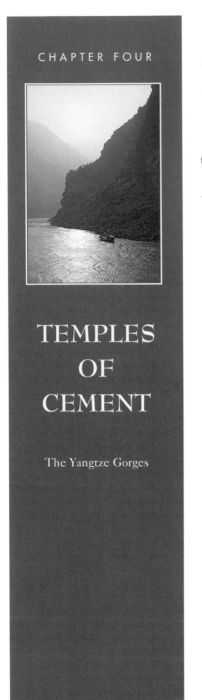

CHAPTER FOUR

TEMPLES
OF
CEMENT

The Yangtze Gorges

From its source high (6,600 metres; 21,653 feet) in the frozen wastes of the Tibetan Plateau, the Yangtze River cleaves the landmass of China clean in half. Flowing 6,300 kilometres (3,914 miles) to its mouth on the East China Sea, it is the third longest river in the world. It carries more water than any river except the Amazon, and it supports a greater population than any other waterway. At least 400 million Chinese — eight per cent of humanity — depend on this river for survival.

In the Yangtze Gorges

The first rice ever to be cultivated may have come from the Yangtze valley: grains of rice 7,000 years old have been discovered in Zhejiang Province, near Shanghai. The Yangtze is to China what the Nile is to Egypt, the Mississippi to North America. Its remote upper reaches are to this day not fully explored. But to the millions who live on the broad Yangtze plain the river is known simply as Chang Jiang — the Long River.

The Yangtze River may be the highway of China, its watershed the nation's breadbasket, but its alter ego is a monster. When the summer rains come and the river swells, half of China crosses its fingers. The floods of 1993, which killed about 3,000 and did eleven billion US dollars' damage, were a minor affair by Yangtze standards. Thirty-three thousand died in the flood of 1954, 142,000 in 1935 and 145,000 in 1931 when three million were left homeless and people had to get around the streets of Wuhan in rowboats for a fortnight. There aren't any accurate records for casualties of the 1870 flood, the worst in 1,000 years, but if it happened again tomorrow, a million people might die.

On 16th July 1966 Mao Zedong took a deep breath and plunged into the waters of the Yangtze at Wuhan. Hundreds of ecstatic youngsters cheered and followed him in. When the headlines burst across the newspapers the following week, it was claimed that Mao had swum 15 kilometres (9 miles) across the river in one hour and five minutes. The idea was to demonstrate that the Great Helmsman still had the capability that some of his recent actions might have led people to suspect he had lost. He wanted to show not only that he still had his hand on the helm, but that he was capable of steering it in any direction he pleased. A few sceptics suggested that this might have had more to do with the strength of the current than with the seventy-two-year-old Chairman's athletic prowess, but their doubts made little difference.

From Wuhan Mao went directly to Beijing, where a month later he greeted a million Red Guards in Tiananmen Square, appearing like a god as the sun came up and the crowd sang 'The East is Red'. He appealed to the youth of the country to go out into the streets and make revolution, to attack their teachers, attack those in authority, attack the very Party he had built with his own hands and which he now believed had lost its revolutionary purity. The Great Proletarian Cultural Revolution had begun.

The orgy of violence that followed enabled Mao to retain paramount control over China until his death ten years later. Perhaps half a million people died as a result of the Cultural Revolution, priceless historic monuments across the country were laid waste and an entire generation turned on its seniors. In a society where respect for age and education had been the most fundamental tenets since the time of Confucius, it is difficult to imagine a more shocking exhortation than Mao's.

In April 1992 the National People's Congress in Beijing approved a motion to begin construction work on the Three Gorges Dam project. The plan is to build a 185-metre (607-foot) high, 2-kilometre (1¼-mile) wide dam above the city of Yichang, which will create a reservoir stretching 600 kilometres (373 miles) upriver to Chongqing. If successful, it will revolutionise the waterway, improving navigation, controlling flooding and generating billions of watts of much-needed electricity. However, even within the Chinese government, support for the dam was not unanimous: in a move that was completely without precedent, one-third of the delegates to the Congress voted against the project.

Control the waters and you control China; neglect the rivers and you have flood, famine and chaos. From the time of the legendary Great Yu in 2300 BC to Deng Xiaoping, every emperor has understood this fundamental principle. If Beijing can pull off the Three Gorges Dam, it will have demonstrated that the mandate of heaven is still the property of the Communist Party.

Everyone knows that the Chinese love a bet, and this one has to be one of the biggest yet. Twenty billion US dollars says that Beijing can whip seven affected provinces and half a dozen competing bureaucracies into line, juggle cutting edge technology with stupendous financial demands, organise massive amounts of labour and complete one of the world's most ambitious engineering schemes to tame Asia's most volatile river, just like the good old days. A million lives says it can't.

* * *

All I can remember of the city of Yichang is concrete, haze, a mile of oily barges tied up along the riverbank and some steep hills half obscured in the murk. Any evidence of the walled city Morrison knew is long gone.

Wen came up to me while I was standing in the lobby of my hotel wondering what to do next. He had a round, open face and was wearing fake patent leather shoes, baggy jeans and a purple cotton jacket. He had some English and was offering me his services as a guide.

'What is there to see in Yichang?'

'We can go and see the dam,' he said.

So we hired bikes and went to see Yichang's number one tourist attraction.

The Gezhouba (Gezhou Dam) lies 4 kilometres (2 miles) west of Yichang and was built, among other things, as a trial run for the Three Gorges Dam. If Three Gorges is built it will dwarf Gezhouba, which at the moment is the biggest dam in China. Work began on Gezhouba in 1970. Between 1972 and 1974 construction was at a complete standstill as major design faults were ironed out. Much of the previous work had to be ripped out and started anew. The entire project was supposed to take five years; it ended up taking twenty. Construction of the Three Gorges Dam is projected to take seventeen years.

Yangtze boats moored at Yichang

Deck-class accommodation on a Yangtze boat

In the Yangtze Gorges

TOP AND BOTTOM: *Farmer in the Yangtze Gorges*

Wen and I got off our bikes and walked on to the concrete road leading across the top. There were a few souvenir shops, and I took a look in one of them. On sale were postcards of the dam, books about the dam, maps of the dam, posters of the dam. I could have gone for a dam teatowel, but they seemed to have sold out.

A Belgian tour group trooped past in cotton pants and sensible hats, and we nodded at each other. Wen and I walked across the wall, looked at the hydropower complex, and walked back again. My senses recorded yellow concrete, brown water and the low hum of electricity.

That night I had dinner with Wen and his friend Li, a wiry man in his mid-twenties who had a slightly electric air about him. We had a few bottles of local beer. On the label was a picture of the dam.

Between mouthfuls of noodles I asked Li, whose English was better than Wen's, about transport upriver. At Yichang Morrison had transferred to a small boat called a *wupan* for the remainder of the river journey. A wupan — which means five boards, as opposed to *sampan*, which means three boards — was a 10-metre (33-foot) sailboat. Immediately above Yichang the Three Gorges begin, a narrow, 240-kilometre (149-mile) long channel through spectacular limestone mountains. In Morrison's day, steam navigation stopped at Yichang. After this, you took a junk, or a wupan, or some other kind of sailboat, and prayed that you wouldn't come to grief in the swirling waters and treacherous rapids.

'Is it possible to hire a wupan to go from here to Chongqing?' I asked Li.

'A what?'

'A wupan. It's a kind of small sailboat. I want to take one to Chongqing.'

At this Li laughed so hard some Gezhouba beer flew out of his nose, hitting the clump of noodles he had been about to shovel into his mouth. It suddenly dawned on me that I hadn't seen a sailboat since the last time I'd been out on Sydney Harbour.

'There is no such thing!' was all he could finally force out.

'Well, what about some other kind of small boat?' I asked, trying to stay serious.

'Yes, yes, of course you can get a small boat.'

'Oh good. What kind of boat?'

'A passenger boat, of course. There are big ones and small ones. The small ones carry about 800 passengers.'

This wasn't getting me anywhere. 'What about a cargo boat? Like the ones I've seen moored along the river.'

'No, no, this is impossible. It is dangerous. The government will never permit it. It will take a long time, and it will be very uncomfortable. Why do you want to travel like this?'

'I've caught plenty of passenger boats already,' I said. 'I want to see how the real Chinese live. I don't care how long it takes.'

'I will ask for you,' he promised. 'But I think it will be difficult.'

The next day I hired a bike and went to meet Li in the new part of Yichang, built on an island in the middle of the river. He hadn't been able to find a boat for me. I wasn't exactly surprised. We rode around for a while.

'This island was formed when they built the dam,' said Li. 'The far stream is where the river was diverted. All these apartments were built to house the dam workers. Before the dam was built, Yichang was a very small place. My parents came here as workers. Now they have a comfortable flat here.'

'What do you think of the Three Gorges Dam?'

'It will be a very good thing. Since the Gezhouba was finished, there is not much work here. The new dam will create a lot of jobs.'

We had reached the opposite side of the island. A barge was moored to the bank. A gang of labourers was unloading coal, carrying it from the hold in little baskets slung from bamboo poles. I took a few photos.

Some of the labourers sat down, and Li started to talk to them.

'These men come from Sichuan,' he said, 'but there is no work there. They are from the country. They are very poor. You can ask them some questions if you like.'

I hesitated. 'How much do they earn?' I said.

'I told you, they are very poor!' Li hit back. 'You wanted to see the real China. Here it is! Ask them some questions!' His face was tense and his voice had a sudden edge to it.

'Coal is everywhere abundant, and there are excellent briquettes for sale, made of a mixture of clay and coal-dust.'

I was embarrassed. I didn't want to sit and ask how miserable these men's lives were.

'Where do they live?' I asked.

'In shacks over there,' Li spat out, with a wave of his hand. 'Six of them sleep in one room.'

'Are they married?'

'Of course not! How can they afford to get married?'

There was an awkward silence for a while.

'What do they think of the West?' I asked, and Li translated.

'They say that in the West there are some very rich people, but that the difference between rich and poor is much greater than in China,' came the reply.

Li was quiet for a while. 'In 1989 I was a senior at college,' he said as we rode towards his flat. 'I led some protests in my city at the time of Tiananmen Square. That was a bad time, but it was long ago. Now I am married with a son. I am an engineer. Being an engineer is not a good job in China. I don't earn much money. I would like to study some more, but I can't afford to. I have my family to think about. Capitalism or communism, I don't care. Now I am a Christian. But I would like to be able to earn some more money.' Li had learned English on his own, and knew words like 'ubiquitous' and expressions like 'kick the bucket'.

We arrived at his flat, provided by his work unit at a nominal rent of 20 yuan a month. It was in a drab six-storey block. The entire island bristled with buildings of identical design, endless hundreds of them. Li gave me a cup of tea, and then Wen arrived. Wen didn't have a work permit for Yichang, which meant he couldn't get a job or a flat. Often he slept over at Li's, he said. If he planned to make it as a tour guide, I couldn't help thinking, he'd picked the wrong city.

We sat around making dumplings, folding minced pork with chives and egg into little squares of dough. It's a traditional thing for guests to do with their hosts, Li told me. I kept botching them.

We drank more Gezhouba beer, and soon Li's wife turned up, smiling, willowy, attractive. She didn't speak English, Li told me, but her English name was Gertrude. I didn't press for an explanation. She disappeared into their tiny kitchen and, in between a long day at work and putting their son to bed, churned out a meal of preserved eggs, pickled radish, stir-fried broccoli with pork, and fried peanuts. We sat down. I kept dropping peanuts from my chopsticks, making little oily stains on my jeans.

'What places should I visit in the Three Gorges?' I asked Li.

'Ah, there is so much history in the Three Gorges, and I can see you like history. There are many famous places. The first one is the home of the poet Qu Yuan, a very famous man in China. Qu Yuan was a great poet and statesman of the Qu Kingdom. He was afraid that the power of the rival Qin Kingdom was becoming too great, but the king would not listen, and he was betrayed at court. So he drowned himself in a river. There is a legend that a giant fish took his body in its mouth and carried it back so it could be buried at his ancestral home in Zigui, at the end of the first gorge, which we call Xiling Gorge. A temple was built here to commemorate him. After Qu Yuan's death, the Qin invaded Qu and destroyed it.'

'When did this happen?'

'About 2,000 years ago.'

'And what will happen to this place when the dam is built?' I asked.

'The site of the temple will go underwater, but they are planning to move the building itself to another site, some kilometres away.'

I found myself contemplating this paradox: that a people so proud of their long history can so readily expunge the ancient traces of that history. The Yangtze Gorges, without a doubt, contain a treasury of archaeological sites that has not yet even been discovered and, if the dam is built, presumably never will be. Or maybe it's not a paradox. Maybe history to the Chinese is something internal, fixed not in monuments and relics but in the mind: a collective consciousness of greatness that acts sometimes as a bedrock, sometimes as a millstone.

'You can visit the Baidi Cheng, the White King Palace, at Fengjie,' Li went on. 'In the time of the Three Kingdoms, Liu Bei attacked the king of Wu, Sun Quan, after Sun had murdered Liu's blood brother. The armies of Wu attacked the armies of Liu while they were camped in the forest by the river, and destroyed them. Liu Bei returned to the Baidi Cheng to die of shame and bitterness. Before he died, he passed his kingdom to his other blood brother, Zhuge Liang, who built defences and fought off the invading Wu army. Zhuge Liang was one of the most famous soldiers of China — even today, the army studies his strategies.'

'And what will happen to this place when they build the dam?' I asked.

'It will be drowned!' he said happily.

We drank beer and played mah-jong till one o'clock. Then I got up to wobble home on my bike. My boat left at five the next morning. Before I left, Li asked me to send him a Bible from Australia. Then he and Gertrude presented me with a little clay tea set.

* * *

Navigating the Yangtze Gorges was the first true adventure of Morrison's trip. In places, the tightness of the course and the sheer weight of water drive the river at speeds up to 30 kilometres (19 miles) per hour. Apart from during a flood, the most dangerous time to sail the Gorges is in winter, when the water is lowest and the rocks and reefs are exposed. This is when Morrison did it.

The only method then known of navigating the Gorges was a combination of sail and sheer human labour. Junks, weighing as much as 100 tonnes, were hauled

中国

up the river by teams of 'trackers' up to 250 strong. A drummer would beat a constant tattoo from the deck of the junk and firecrackers would be let off for good luck as the trackers strained along narrow paths incised into the jagged cliffs, sometimes without room for a person to stand upright. If a junk missed its course, trackers could be jerked into the river, never to be seen again; a tracker who lost his footing was liable to be dragged bouncing across the rocks, and left to nurse his broken body by the riverbank. A contemporary of Morrison's estimated that one in forty junks was lost in the rapids.

A wupan, light, flexible and tough, was far safer than a junk if you could get one. Even so, Morrison was soaked to the skin more than once in the freezing February waters; his boat was almost lost in the first big rapid, and later nearly smashed to pieces by a junk speeding out of control down the river. A Yangtze boatman had to know every rock in the river, every current, eddy and stream. The system of trackers plus sail had been in use on the Yangtze Gorges — for practical purposes the only route connecting the vast wealth of the central province of Sichuan to the immense population of the east — since at least the Song dynasty (AD 960–1279).

In 1900 a steamer owned by a British entrepreneur became the first boat to make the trip from Yichang to Chongqing under its own power. Within a decade, a regular steamer service had begun on the Gorges. Although the system of trackers hauling junks only finally disappeared in the 1950s, an era had ended.

* * *

The beginning of a boat trip is still marked with a fury of firecrackers, but instead of the Yichang city wall and the sterns of countless junks we now had only to pass the massive ship lock of the Gezhouba. I slept through this part.

When I woke, we were in a different world. Two enormous slabs of grey rock closed us in, squeezing the river like some gigantic wine press. The boat's diesels strained and growled against the force of the current, and the foghorn blew continuously. Every few minutes, another boat, a practical green and grey steel construction just like ours, would race past in the opposite direction, disappearing fast into the misty haze that rose from the water. I walked up to the top deck for a better view, where Chinese tourists 'oohed' and 'aahed' and pointed out details I could only guess at. Were we passing the rocks that look like the sword and the book on the art of war? Or the rocks that are said to resemble the four characters from the mythological story *Monkey*? Or perhaps the rocks that are supposed to resemble a cow's liver and a horse's lung?

After an hour or two the gorge opened out. Little white farmhouses appeared, perched precariously on the slopes, amid orchards of mandarins, plums and peaches. Narrow terraces had been hacked out of every conceivable space.

We were at the village of Sandouping, near where Morrison met a former cocky*
from South Australia, married to a Chinese woman, in charge of an outpost of the
customs service. On the north bank, far off in the haze, a great gash in the red earth
resembled a kids' sandpit. Yellow and green tip-up trucks looked like Tonka toys
as they trundled back and forth, minute against the giant earthworks. Humans
were dwarfed to invisibility. We had reached the site of the Three Gorges Dam.

The landscape took on a surreal air. From here on it was impossible to look at
anything without thinking that in a few years' time it would be underwater. If the
dam is completed, 104 towns and two cities will be drowned. Fifteen thousand
hectares (370,066 acres) of farmland will be submerged. The 'landscape of red hills
and rich green pastures, of groves of bamboo and cypress, of pretty little
farmhouses with overhanging eaves and picturesque temples in wooded glens' that
Morrison described, will disappear for ever. At least a million people — many of
them doubtless descendants of the trackers who toiled along the banks just fifty
years ago — will have to move.

I don't think anyone questions Beijing's ability to shift vast numbers of people
from one part of the country to another. But there's something else. The Yangtze
bears an enormous amount of silt — about four per cent of all the silt discharged by
all the rivers in the world. If the Three Gorges Dam is completed, there is a very
real possibility that within a century or two the entire 600-kilometre (373-mile)
reach from Chongqing to Yichang will have turned into a giant mud bath.
Nobody can say for sure that it will happen. But nobody can say for sure that
it won't, either.

I got off the boat at Zigui and went to look at the temple to the poet–statesman
Qu Yuan, whose dire warnings about the rise of Qin power were ignored by a
complacent king and his fawning courtiers until it was too late, and Qu himself had
gone to a watery grave.

When I'd climbed, sweating, up the hill to the shrine, bought a can of Coke
from the little stall by the entrance, and got my breath back, I took a proper look at
the building and saw that it wasn't ancient at all. Bits of it might have been old, but
most of it looked twentieth century. It is this amalgam of stone and cement that
the government is going to move up the hill at vast expense, while the village
where Qu Yuan was born and — so the legend goes — tilled the family rice field, is
inundated.

A troop of Chinese tourists overtook me as they rushed around the monument.
It didn't matter to them that there wasn't much to see inside; doubtless they'd all
known the story of Qu Yuan since childhood. They hadn't come here to learn, they
had come to bow before an icon. And then it finally dawned on me. The dam

---

* *Small landholder*

wasn't about obliterating history, any more than the Cultural Revolution had been. It was about reinventing it. It was to be a shrine to Deng Xiaoping, who is about to die, and Li Peng, Premier of China, the Soviet-trained electrical engineer who blackened his name throughout China and the world when he ordered tanks into Tiananmen Square in the early hours of 4th June 1989. These men weren't indifferent to history. They were obsessed with it.

If he could come back today, what would Qu Yuan counsel them about the Three Gorges Dam? Would they listen? I don't know. But if I were him, I'd be getting ready for another dunking.

* * *

The next afternoon, I was on another throbbing steel kerosene tin of a boat sailing up Witches Gorge. The clouds had darkened and a drizzle was falling; on the bank opposite I could see the remains of the footpath once used by the trackers. I was surrounded by a crowd of middle school teachers, on holiday from Tianjin.

'What is your country?' asked one of them as she offered me a mandarin.

'Aodaliya,' I said.

'Do you think China is beautiful?' she asked me.

'Well, parts of it are,' I replied, because I'm a hopeless liar. 'And how do you like the Sanxia — the Three Gorges?'

She smiled at this. 'Before I came, I thought it would be wonderful. But now I am here, I think it is just so-so.'

Her candour surprised me. Up to now I had been trying hard to convince myself that the Gorges really were all they were cracked up to be, but I had to admit that she was right. The mountains are almost always obscured by haze, the towns are grey and the river — well, the river is the drain of half of China, and it looks like it. The grandeur of the Three Gorges is an exaggeration, a myth perpetuated by fine brush paintings of misty crags, and tourist brochures and the picture on the back of the 5-yuan note.

But then myths usually are more beautiful than reality.

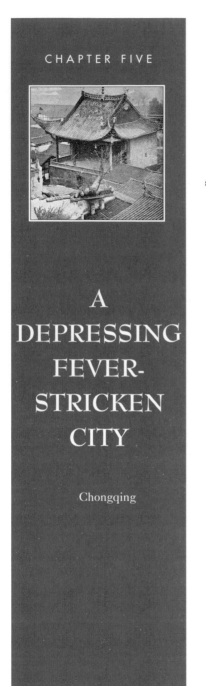

CHAPTER FIVE

A DEPRESSING FEVER-STRICKEN CITY

Chongqing

The first thing I had to do when I got to Chongqing was climb a staircase leading from the riverbank to the city itself. The reason for this is pretty obvious — if the city were actually built by the water, then it would disappear in the first flood of the year. Every town on the Yangtze has this problem. In most cases these staircases are about as high as the walls of a Yangtze gorge, and only marginally less steep. On this particular day they were also slippery with drizzle.

'Temple theatre in Chungking'

As I was carrying three stills cameras and lenses, a video camera and a backpack stuffed with books, notes, film, winter clothes, sleeping bag and a big jar of Nescafe-and-Coffee-Mate, about 30 kilograms (66 pounds) in all, I wasn't at all sorry that this would be the last time I'd have to do it.

Or so I thought. Over the preceding weeks, everyone I'd come across who spoke a bit of English had impressed upon me the fact that Chongqing was a mountain city. That sounds nice, I'd thought, picturing an idyllic hinterland of lush hills, or perhaps grand vistas of snow-capped peaks marching off to the horizon. Something like Kathmandu, or perhaps Srinagar, with a bit of luck. In other words, I'd assumed all along that 'mountain city' meant that the city was in the mountains. In fact, it meant that the mountains were in the city.

Unlike Wuhan, though, no one, not even people who lived there had claimed that Chongqing was a 'beautiful city'.

If Chinese is a difficult language for Westerners to get a grip on, the various different systems for transliterating it into the Roman alphabet don't help. The city that was called Chungking in Morrison's day is spelled 'Chongqing' under the more recent system known as Pinyin. Not that that gives any better idea how the name is pronounced by the city's inhabitants: about the closest spelling you'll ever get in English is something like 'Choong-ching'. But I'm sure modern-day scholars have as good a reason for rendering a *ch* sound as a 'q' as their predecessors did for making it into a 'k'.

At least Pinyin sometimes gets a little closer to the mark. The name Peking, for example, has always been pronounced *Beijing* by the Chinese. If many Westerners mispronounced it for generations, it's because they didn't know that the 'P' was supposed to stand for a 'B' and the 'k' for a 'j'. Similarly, the city of Nanking is really Nanjing. On the other hand, the name of the last imperial dynasty to rule China is nowadays spelled 'Qing', but in fact it is pronounced *Ch'ing*, which is how it was written under the old system. Figure that out.

I went downtown. There were the inevitable cranes and construction sites where a thousand busy bodies hammered, piled and wheeled things about, and a misty haze so thick I could barely see across the river. The centre of Chongqing is marked by the Jiefang Bei — the Liberation Monument, a monstrous hexagonal phallus in cream and brown. Surrounding it on every side were billboards, department stores, crowds and street vendors carrying long poles that dangled with everything from balloons to brassieres. I wandered into a camera store to see what they had; it was reassuring to know that if someone nicked my kit, I could buy a brand-new Hasselblad straight off the shelf. Assuming I could afford one, which I couldn't.

A young German was also in there, and we said hello. He was from a national badminton team, visiting Chongqing for a competition which the Chinese were hosting. Later I noted down the main points of what he told me.

1. The sun never shines in Chongqing. 2. There is nothing to see in Chongqing. 3. No Western tourists come to Chongqing. 4. His badminton team came bottom of the competition.

'The Chinese players — fantastic!' he said with awe. Then he had to go, off on a prearranged group tour. It was the first conversation I'd had with a foreigner since leaving Shanghai. I'm glad I didn't know then that it would be more than a month before I had my next one.

At least, I thought, I'll be able to find a book in English here. Every big Chinese city has a foreign language bookstore, more for the benefit of Chinese students than for visiting foreigners. In Shanghai I'd managed to pick up a couple of volumes of Lu Xun's short stories, but even these masterpieces of twentieth-century Chinese literature were wearing a little thin now that I was reading them for the third time.

I found the bookstore. It was closed for renovations.

Chongqing, Morrison wrote, is 'a depressing fever-stricken city where the sun is never seen from November to June and blazes with an unendurable fierceness from July to October'. He would probably say the same thing today, except that the Yangtze mist is now leavened with a generous helping of sulphur-laden smog. Even in Morrison's day, coal was a major source of power in the area. It's poor quality, but there's plenty of it. The difference nowadays is that it is used to drive vast chemical, pharmaceutical, machine building, steel, metallurgical, food processing and textile enterprises, many of which are now thirty-plus years old. Belching smokestacks blot the horizon in every direction.

Much like Los Angeles, Chongqing sits in the middle of an amphitheatre of hills which hold in the pollution, slowly strangling the city. The air pollution in many Chinese cities exceeds the World Health Organisation recommended maximum by factors of five or six, and Chongqing is one of the worst. In 1894 many people in Chongqing would have been lucky to get one square meal a day. In 1994 they're not starving any more, but they're breathing in a toxic soup.

Chongqing is built on a peninsula, a finger of land pointing at the confluence of the Yangtze and Jialing Rivers. The city spreads across the north and south banks, connected by bridges and cable cars, but the real metropolis is on the great crown of rock in the centre. Here Morrison found temples and rich mansions with courtyards, pagodas and city walls and missions with their churches and hospitals.

World War II took care of all that. In 1938 the Guomindang government, led by Chiang Kai-shek, pulled back to Chongqing in the face of the Japanese advance, there to form an uneasy alliance with the communists while they organised a resistance. Like the Russians in the face of Napoleon's armies, the Chinese preferred strategic withdrawal to direct confrontation, hoping to outlast the Japanese, to exhaust them with the vastness of their country. The retreat followed exactly the route I had just taken, moving up the Yangtze as in turn Shanghai, Nanjing and Wuhan fell to the invader, and the vast bulk of China's industrial capacity along with them. In Nanjing, the occupation was accompanied by an orgy of murder, rape and wanton destruction that defies imagination.

Trucks, carts, boats and waves of human labour were pressed into service as much of China moved west, taking with it everything it could carry, harassed by bombers all the way. Universities full of students were uprooted and re-established themselves behind the barrier of the mountains. Whole factories were disassembled and loaded into fleets of junks, which then battled their way up the Gorges. Machines were carried, piece by piece, or rolled on wooden rollers by barefoot coolies for hundreds of kilometres.

Wartime Chongqing was a city bulging with refugees, infested with rats and with no protection from the frequent bombing raids. 'The Japanese preferred moonlit nights for their calls, when from their base in Hankow [Wuhan] they could follow the silver banner of the Yangtze up to its confluence with the Jialing, which identified the capital in a way no blackout could obscure,' wrote the American journalist Edgar Snow, who visited the city in 1941. With virtually no air force, the Chinese had no option but to sit and take it for three long years. The city was smashed, but it survived. As it had many times in the past, the fertile province of Sichuan acted as a fortress, a redoubt protected by near-impenetrable mountains and the Yangtze Gorges, in which to sit out an invasion and plan a counterattack.

According to Edgar Snow, there has been a city at the site of present-day Chongqing for over 4,000 years. To look at it now, you'd think the whole thing was thrown up in the fifties. Which, in fact, it was.

So much for downtown Chongqing. The only hope I had of finding some remnants of the city Morrison saw, I now realised, was to search for the places that appear in the photos in his book. It was time to do a bit of detective work.

The first of the photos was of a place called Fu-to-kuan, which Morrison describes as a fort on top of a hill 4 miles (6 kilometres) west of the city, which he passed as he left Chongqing on his way to Kunming. Here, the peninsula narrows to an isthmus, so that with a fort guarding the only land access, the city would have been impregnable. The photo showed an elaborate arch in front of a crenellated wall and gateway with a double roof and curved eaves.

> Set in the face of the cliff is a gigantic image of Buddha. Massive stone portals, elaborately carved, and huge commemorative tablets cut from single blocks of stone and deeply engraved, here adorn the highway. The archways have been erected by command of the Emperor, but at the expense of their relatives, to the memory of virtuous widows who have refused to remarry, or who have sacrificed their lives on the death

of their husbands. Happy are those whose names are thus recorded, for not only do they obtain ten thousand merits in heaven, as well as the Imperial recognition of the Son of Heaven on earth; but as an additional reward their souls may, on entering the world a second time, enjoy the indescribable felicity of inhabiting the bodies of men.

Fu-to-kuan, or Futoguan, sounded like quite a place. I bought a map of Chongqing from a street vendor for 5 mao. It was entirely in Chinese, but it didn't matter, I could see the narrowest point in the isthmus. I jumped on a bus and asked the conductor to tell me when we reached Futoguan. Twenty minutes later, I was there.

I struggled up the steep hillside, sweating in the close air. There was forest and a decaying stone path and, at the top, a citadel of perpendicular cliff, big, grey and solid as a battleship. I followed the cliff east, heading back in the direction of the city. There were a few caves with pillars and carvings, but they were made of concrete: another recent restoration job. After half an hour, I came to the sharp end of the battleship. An old couple had a little stall where they were selling tea, peanuts and pumpkin seeds. I had a cup of tea and showed them both the photo, asking if they knew the place. They seemed to have an argument, and both shook their heads. They then smiled at me, and pointed in opposite directions. I paid for my tea.

I rounded the corner and followed the cliffs on the other side. There was a large statue of the Buddha set into the rock high up above my head, and some women were praying and lighting incense to it. Now, I thought, I'm getting somewhere. There were a few inscriptions in the rock, and then some stairs leading to the top of the hill. At the top, the wall and fortress had disappeared without a trace. In their place stood the concrete bunkers and steel towers of the Chongqing television station.

But what about the memorial arches? I walked across the top of the hill and down the other side. There were some apartment blocks and an enormous hospital. I came to the main road, which must have been the route Morrison walked. There were truck yards, hardware shops and a constant banging and clanging from more construction sites. The air reeked of exhaust. I waded through this depressing bit of urban sprawl until I found a road branching back off toward the hill, and took it. I was hungry, sweaty and tired.

Suddenly there was a vision on the footpath in front of me. She was in a body-hugging purple dress with black stockings and high-heeled shoes. Her hair was long, black and luxuriant and her delicate face was made up as perfectly powder-white as a geisha in an eighteenth-century woodblock. She turned around and smiled. I smiled back.

I reached the top of the hill again. I had no idea where to turn next. I looked around and there she was. 'Can I help you?' she said in that gorgeous singsong.

Her name was Li and she was an announcer on Chongqing television. I showed her the book and explained my problem. 'Oh, you are a reporter also!' she said. Not surprisingly, she had never heard of Morrison.

Then she looked at the picture and shook her head. Her English was self-taught, and didn't quite run to 'memorial archway'.

We went to meet someone called Deng, who was a news editor at the station. He was a smooth-looking gentleman, and I was disappointed to discover that he was Li's boyfriend. We all had a cup of tea in his office, and Li translated as we chatted. She took out an English–Chinese dictionary and looked up 'memorial', then 'archway', and squealed with comprehension when she realised what it was. Then she said something to Deng.

'Deng knows where this place is,' she said. 'Come, we will show you.'

We walked down the same footpath to the cliffs with the Buddha statue and the inscriptions.

'There were many memorial arches and statues of the Buddha here,' Deng told me through Li. He was pointing to some gaping holes in the cliff which obviously once held statues; in one of them, small figures which had once sat behind the main statue still remained. There were fresh sticks of incense at the base.

'Was it destroyed during the war?' I asked.

'*Bu shi. Ee juo liu liu.*' 1966, he was saying. I took his meaning. That was the year the Cultural Revolution began.

'There were many of these arches here. But at that time they were all broken,' said Li. 'That new statue was put there in the 1980s.'

It was five o'clock, and far too murky to take a picture. I would have to come back. Li and Deng walked with me to the bottom of the hill.

The next photograph was called simply 'A temple theatre in Chungking' and showed a complex that included a stone platform and some fine old buildings with tiled roofs. Morrison doesn't mention it in his text, so I knew it would be hard to find. I showed it around the staff of my hotel and asked if the building still existed and, if not, where it had stood. The consensus was that it had disappeared, and that a cinema now stood in its place. The spot was pointed out to me on my map, right in the centre of town, near the Liberation Monument.

The next morning, I found the 5–1 Cinema. Its facade was all reflective glass, chrome pipes and pillars. It was definitely one of Chongqing's flashier movie houses, but I couldn't help thinking I would have preferred the original. Jensen's picture brought to mind Chinese opera, with crashing cymbals and wailing horns, flowing robes and mincing steps, boys dressed as girls, powdery make-up and piping falsetto and coiffure verging on the extreme. I could picture the dissipated patrons of old Chungking, foggy with opium, sitting and spitting and sipping their tea in their tasselled hats and brocades as they watched their favourite operas into the small hours of the morning, chatting to their friends and commenting on the nuances of the performance, while beggars, vendors and sedan chair coolies waited outside.

I strolled across to look at what was showing. A big red banner was draped across the front of the building; the number 100 was the only bit of it I could read. Then I saw the posters advertising a picture about the life of Chairman Mao. There was a battlefield scene and an intense-looking young Mao. Bio pics about Mao are as perennial in China as Woody Allen films are in the West — I remember reading somewhere that there is an actor who makes his entire living just by playing Mao — but this one was special. It had been produced to commemorate Mao's hundredth birthday, which was coming up on 26th December, and was showing in every city I visited.

When Mao died in September 1976 and his faction, the Gang of Four, were ejected from power by Deng Xiaoping, the Communist Party was presented with a sticky problem: how to acknowledge Mao's undoubtedly great achievement in unifying China and bringing the Party to power, while at the same time dissociating itself from his horrendous mistakes and abuses? They toyed with various formulas, including one that would have said Mao was mostly right before a certain point sometime in the 1950s, and mostly wrong thereafter. It took them years, but finally they came up with this piece of analysis: Mao was seventy per cent right, and thirty per cent wrong. With this formula in place, he could now safely be turned into an icon.

* * *

By afternoon the atmosphere had thickened again. I climbed Pipa Shan, the highest hill in Chongqing where, according to Morrison, the German Commissioner of Customs had a house, in front of which was a temple. There was nothing up there now but a pavilion and a couple of shops selling souvenirs. Looking at the view, I could barely see the tops of the city skyscrapers through the mist.

Heading back down the stone stairs in the drizzle, I slipped on one of the steps and landed hard on my bum, grazing the heels of both my hands. I cursed at the top of my voice and shed a few tears, more from frustration than pain. I had come thousands of kilometres in search of Morrison's China — so where the bloody hell was it? I was fully halfway across China, and of all the things he'd described I'd found a couple of landscapes, and that was it. If this was how it was going to be, I might as well turn around and go home now.

I went back to my hotel and bought some Chinese brandy, fierce, throat-searing stuff in an opaque green bottle with a gold label. Before long the hall attendant's boyfriend came and joined me. For a while we just grinned at each other like idiots and drank in silence. By the time we were halfway through the bottle, we were singing 'Oh Susanna' in Chinese and English. As I only know the chorus, there must have been some improvising going on, but I can't really remember. By the time we'd finished it, I felt distinctly sick.

When I woke up the next morning and looked out of the window, I couldn't believe my eyes. The cloud was separating into long thin fingers shot with strips of pale blue, and the sun was shining shyly. Ignoring the pounding in my skull, I hauled my clothes on, grabbed my camera and rushed outside.

I had one photo left to get, a shot of the Chongqing peninsula from the south bank of the Yangtze. From my map, I knew exactly where to go. In the original picture, the south bank looks positively rural. Now it is the outskirts of the city,

Tea drinkers, Chongqing

and once I got out of the cab I found myself walking through market gardens and people's backyards, past little boys spinning tops and old men sitting on their front porches sipping tea and smoking long thin pipes with tiny bowls. Rural China was beckoning sweetly, but first I had to get the picture. When I finally found something approximating the viewpoint, I remember thinking that the sunshine and clarity were wonderful. But when I see the picture now, it looks as soupily filthy as an average day in Los Angeles.

The next day the smog was as thick as ever. I picked up my pack and headed for the bus station.

TOP AND BOTTOM: 'The city of Chungking from the opposite bank of the Yangtse'

中国

TOP AND BOTTOM: *Old and new in Chongqing*

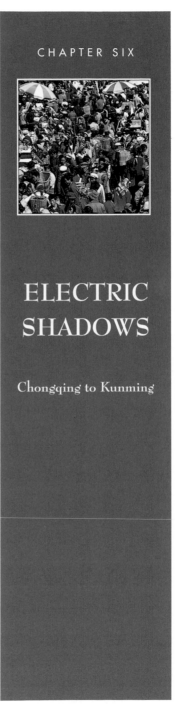

CHAPTER SIX

ELECTRIC SHADOWS

Chongqing to Kunming

For three days I headed west through country that might have been interesting if I had been able to see it. Sichuan has a reputation for frequently being covered in thick cloud and haze. 'When the sun shines, the dogs bark,' goes a local proverb. A canopy of cloud lay over a country of sandstone as richly red as Central Australia, but this landscape was crowded with humanity. Sichuan is the most fertile province in China, a place where any plant found anywhere in China can be grown. It is home to a cool hundred million people, and I was in the thick of it.

Village market

Zhaotong

中国

Zhaotong

Gongshan

Dawn over mountains near Zhaotong

中国

'Mountain coolies, such as the tea-carriers, bear the weight of their burden on their shoulders, carrying it as we do a knapsack, not in the ordinary Chinese way, with a pliant carrying pole. They are all provided with a short staff, which has a transverse handle curved like a boomerang, and with this they ease the weight off the back, while standing at rest.'

'Fierce door-gods guarded against the admission of evil spirits. Brave indeed must be the spirits who venture within reach of such fierce bearded monsters, armed with such desperate weapons, as were here represented.'

For three days it was like travelling through a surreal underworld. The sky was a low vault of whitish grey melding indefinably with the ancient earth. The dark dusty redness of the soil lay all around, creeping up the whitewashed walls of the houses, the faded blue clothes of the farmers, every leaf and every tree trunk, as if the scene had been sculpted from it. It was like being inside a diorama in a museum, caged in by the sky like a glass case murky with schoolchildren's fingerprints, a primal scene from a geography teacher's dream.

Farmers, half obscured in the haze, tilled the paddy fields, knee-deep in muck. Low hills and shallow valleys had been parcelled up into intricate terraces without an inch to spare. Every so often, I would see a farmhouse or a grove of cypress or a drooping clump of bamboo forming a tiny island in this sea of cultivation as we growled and bounced along the rough road.

Sometimes a bus would come the other way, looming through the murk like a blubbery whale, a huge rubber sac wobbling on its roof. I soon realised that these buses had been converted to run on natural gas which, along with coal, is abundant in the area. Instead of petrol stations there are natural gas stations, and there's no need for a fuel gauge — all the driver has to do is crane his head out the window to see how full the bag is. Which some of them were inclined to do while steering the bus full tilt around a blind corner, I noted with some anxiety.

At the city of Yibin, which was called Suifu in Morrison's time, I joined the Yangtze again, and the next day followed the river to a town which didn't exist in Morrison's day but which has inherited the name of Suifu. Why this is, I don't know, but it was very confusing at the time! The hotel I stayed in that night had a satellite dish that piped Western consumerism into every room. The hotel manager proudly switched on my television, flipped the channel to MTV and left me to it. I was so desperate for a bit of familiar culture, I would have watched anything.

Then I flipped over to Star TV, Rupert Murdoch's station, coming out of Hong Kong. An old episode of 'Richmond Hill' was starting up. This was followed by an hour of 'The Flying Doctors', with a story about a woman who is reunited with her long lost daughter. Do Australians *really* talk like that? I tried to remember. Or were this lot just playing up to the outback cliché? At that moment the horrible realisation dawned on me that Australia's most significant cultural export is probably the soap opera.

So this was the long-awaited satellite TV revolution. Fifty-seven channels of Euro-American junk, twenty-four hours a day, or as long as the power is on. If it's what Asia really wants, then I guess it's no more than it deserves. But if it's not what Asia really wants — well, bad luck folks, because you're going to get it anyway.

I sat up and watched all night.

* * *

For two months I had been travelling more or less straight across China. The next morning I got up and turned left. Away from the Yangtze and out of Sichuan, out of the heartland and into the badlands. Or so most Han Chinese would have you believe. I was entering Yunnan Province.

Before leaving Chongqing, I had fronted up at the China International Travel Service — the government tourist agency with a deservedly lousy reputation — to ask if I could travel this road. As far as I knew, it was still closed to foreigners, as many of the remoter and poorer parts of China are.

'Yes, you can go there, no problem,' said the officer, once I had finally induced him to pay me some attention. 'It has just been opened. You will probably be the first tourist to visit it. But why do you want to go there?' he said with a grimace. 'This trip will be horrible!'

Part of the reason why the Chinese have traditionally regarded their country as the Middle Kingdom is that the Han heartland is surrounded by a periphery largely inhabited by peoples less technologically advanced than themselves. Peoples like the Mongols, the Tibetans, the Vietnamese, the Kazakhs, the Thais and dozens of others. As the Han Chinese expand, the minorities take to the hills. It's been happening for millennia. It's still happening.

From Suifu the road began to climb. The air was miraculously clear after a sudden shower, and the view was limitless. Steep ridges of olive green struggled skywards before giving up halfway on chalky yellow walls of sheer rock. Racing streams glistened silver in the sunlight as they worked their way down from hidden valleys locked behind these immense natural buttresses, joining the grey torrent in the gloomy gorge hundreds of metres below. Farmhouses were notched into the slopes virtually to the base of the cliffs, their terraced fields clinging like wet clothes to the face of the mountain. Further down, cosy hamlets nestled among groves of fir and cedar in happier spots by the river. It was grand like Yosemite and broodingly empty like the Blue Mountains near Sydney, with just the occasional pencil-thin waterfall to remind me that I was in China.

The road was a primitive yellow scar, twisting its way up the steep pass. The towns fell away as we climbed, the houses thinned, and finally it was just the bus battling the grade with a deafening roar, the passengers dozing or smoking or talking; I was by the window, hair thick with dust, goggle-eyed with awe. In the middle of the afternoon we pulled into a town called Daguan, which means 'great fortress', a name which made up in accuracy for what it lacked in originality.

Finding a room was easy. I just asked in shops, using the carefully practised word '*luguan*'. In Chinese there are about five words for 'hotel', depending on your budget, but in a small town like Daguan, these distinctions didn't really matter.

A woman showed me my room, which was decorated like a cut-price bridal suite, with pink mosquito nets, spangles on the ceiling and an elaborate plastic headboard for the bed, and asked me upstairs for a cup of tea. I sat on the terrace as she assailed me with a constant stream of friendly questions, about half of which I understood and a quarter of which I could answer. One of these was '*Ni wei shenme zheli lai?*' — 'Why have you come here?' With my limited vocabulary, how could I even begin to explain?

Meanwhile her three children had surrounded me, and were jumping up and down shouting '*Wai guo ren! Wai guo ren!*' — 'Foreigner! Foreigner!' The view was like one of those mass-produced paintings that you see in milk bars, except it was real.

An old woman with bound feet

中国

I went to get some pictures in the late afternoon light. At the entrance to the hotel, a little posse of children was waiting in ambush. As I walked down the street trying to look nonchalant, they were joined by an increasing number of adults. I walked faster. They walked faster. I slowed down, they slowed down. I stopped, they stopped. Sunning herself on a doorstep was an old lady with bound feet — a common enough sight in Morrison's day, but increasingly rare nowadays as the practice ceased in most parts of China after the 1911 revolution. In remote areas such as this, though, it may have continued for quite some time longer.

I motioned at the camera, and she smiled and nodded. But the crowd had blocked out the light, to say nothing of the spontaneity of the subject. I don't mind being a walking TV set for a while, but this was getting a bit wearing. I turned around and said, '*Zou!*' — 'Go!' Everyone smiled. They were five deep in a semicircle at my back. Somebody in the crowd said, '*Zou!*' and laughed. Nobody moved. I pointed the camera at a small boy. He giggled and ran away. Everyone else stood right where they were.

I gave up and went home, sitting on the terrace as the sunset turned the cliffs from gold to amber to sienna to a colour that wasn't so much a colour as a subtle suggestion of ashy mauve, and then finally to looming black humps against the starry sky. Then I went down for my rice and beer.

The next morning the gloom had descended again. After a final climactic hair-raising climb over the steepest switchbacks of the lot, the bus crested the range. As if by magic, the haze cleared as soon as we lumbered over the top. Looking back north, a quilt of mist smothered the landscape as far as the horizon; to the south, the sky was a clear, deep blue. I thought of my Chinese lessons, and remembered Tanya telling me that Yunnan meant 'south of the clouds' — *yun* being 'clouds' and *nan* being 'south'. The Chinese, I realised, have a penchant for literal place names.

We started rolling down the other side, and fields and houses soon appeared again. It was a different world: the land had come alive with colour. I felt like Judy Garland in *The Wizard of Oz*.

Trees lined the road, shedding autumn leaves of russet and honey. Each house was a courtyard enclosed by ochre mud bricks and roofed with tiles the colour of slate, the walls splashed with yellow, red and olive where maize, chillies and tobacco were draped to dry in the warm sun. Little old women tottered by, already in their padded winter jackets of deepest indigo, and the fields were alive with people as entire villages collected the golden rice stubble. The hills and roads and riverbanks were red, red, red, and the blue of the sky was almost miraculous.

A couple of days later I got to Zhaotong, halfway to Kunming, and collapsed into bed with a fever that probably owed as much to exhaustion as anything else. For two days I lay there with little to do but ponder my inadequacy. Morrison had walked — *walked* — from Chongqing to here, a distance of about 500 kilometres (300 miles), uphill practically all of the way, in just eighteen days. He had rested for a day in Zhaotong before pressing on.

On the first night I woke to what I thought at first was a delirious vision. He was standing by my bed, and he was wearing high-heeled elastic-sided shoes, blue track suit pants two sizes too small with red and white stripes, a crimson jumper and a baggy leather jacket. His hair was an unkempt globe of grizzled steel wool surrounding his fortyish features.

'G'die, mite,' he said.

'What??'

'G'die. My nime is Georgie. Can I help you? Where do you come from?'

'I come from Australia.'

'Oh, Australia. I have been there. Darling Harbour, in eighty-eight. We put on an exhibition there. Here, would you like this? You must be hungry,' he said, holding out a jar of preserved pineapple.

'Thanks,' I said. In Zhaotong, Morrison had stayed with a Scottish missionary called Dymond who had given him oatmeal cakes with Devonshire cream and blackberry jam. And what did I get? A Strine-speaking sartorial disaster and some watery pineapple. Perhaps Morrison didn't have it so bad after all.

But Georgie kept me sane those couple of days, bringing me water and instant noodles and talking to me. I have never been so alone as in those months I spent in central China, and I don't particularly want to be again. I'm grateful to Georgie.

Georgie was gay, and I think he would have been keen if I hadn't been sick. He was working as an interpreter for a couple of British engineers who were in Zhaotong to lend their expertise to a large tobacco factory which also owned the hotel we were staying in. I never saw these men, but I once heard their English accents echoing in the hall outside as they talked of football, while I lay in bed wondering if I was dreaming.

The next day I felt a bit better and sat up in bed going through Morrison's description of Zhaotong. In 1894 the town was a centre for the opium trade, which played a crucial part in Yunnan's economy. In 1994 the government tobacco monopoly is the largest and most profitable industry in China, a nation which produces and consumes more tobacco than any other. Much of this tobacco is grown in Yunnan. Morrison's chapter is titled 'The City of Chaotong; with some remarks on its Poverty, Infanticide, Selling Female Children into Slavery, Tortures, and the Chinese Insensibility to Pain'. Obviously he didn't have a completely positive experience here either.

Let me give an example of the state of development in this area in Morrison's day. From Chongqing to Kunming is a distance of perhaps 800 kilometres (497 miles), and the road Morrison followed is the most direct route, a highway that had been in use for centuries. Yet when the French completed the Hanoi–Kunming railway in 1908, such was the state of this path that people who wanted to travel from Chongqing to Kunming found it faster and safer, and certainly more comfortable, to sail down the Yangtze to Shanghai, change boats and head for Hanoi, and then take the train from Hanoi to Kunming, a detour of, at a guess, somewhere between 5,000 and 6,000 kilometres (3,000 and 4,000 miles).

When the Indian subcontinent collided with the Asian landmass and drove Tibet from the bottom of the ocean to the roof of the world some forty million years ago, creating the biggest and highest plateau on earth, the Yunnan–Guizhou Tableland was shrugged off the edge, like an outhouse with a corrugated-iron roof. The whole of China's south-west flank crinkled into a mountainous tableland that is rich in resources but isolated by powerful natural barriers on every side. It is beautiful, temperate and, by Chinese standards, underpopulated. It grows the best tea, coffee and tobacco in China; 100 years ago, it also grew the best opium. In other words, life there could be pretty enjoyable if you weren't too busy scratching an existence out of the stubborn mountain soil.

Yunnan's problem in Morrison's day wasn't so much the lack of roads; it was that, unlike most other parts of China, it doesn't have any sea ports or navigable rivers. For its administrators it was also a long way from Peking and the centre of the action, a hardship post where the main responsibility was keeping the scruffy barbarians in line, and whose main advantage was that you could line your pockets with minimal supervision before getting back up north.

Yunnan got its first motor road in 1938. In 1994 the province is laced with them, holding together a riot of ethnicity like a string bag full of tropical fruit — busted-up one-truck-wide dirt roads hugging hair-raising mountain slopes in many places, but roads nevertheless.

As he travelled the route, Morrison saw famine, infanticide and slavery, theft, extortion and plague. The fabric of Chinese society, an antique brocade of faded splendour, was shredding to tatters before his very eyes. 'Trouble, serious trouble, will begin in China in the near future, for the time must be fast approaching when the effete and alien dynasty now ruling China — the Manchu Dynasty — shall be overthrown, and a Chinese Emperor shall rule on the throne of China,' wrote Morrison towards the end of his book.

Seventeen years later, an explosion in Wuhan touched off the revolution that would put an inglorious end to 2,000 years of imperial rule. But it wasn't much of a revolution. True to the age-old pattern, China underwent a period of chaos and division before being reunited by a new dynasty. As usual, the outlying provinces were the first to go. In 1916, disgusted by the plan of the first President of the Chinese Republic to have himself crowned emperor, Yunnan seceded, signalling the fragmentation of China into a collection of states ruled by warlords who would fight among themselves for a decade while Japanese generals rubbed their hands with glee. That vainglorious statesman was Yuan Shikai, and his political adviser was one George Ernest Morrison. (Morrison, to his credit, opposed Yuan's plan to have himself crowned emperor.)

* * *

That evening I was sitting up with Georgie watching TV. After what seemed like hours of basketball, a program came on which I had already seen a couple of times, and which had intrigued me. It was called *A Native of Beijing in New York City*, and it had been shot in New York on what looked like a single Hi-8 camera by someone with an itchy zoom finger. Most of the characters were Chinese, but some were American, and there were flashes of English, with subtitles. There seemed to be a lot of getting in and out of big black cars, and earnest discussion of commercial law.

I asked Georgie what it was about, and he launched into a long description of a convoluted plot which I had trouble following. But as far as I could tell, it was the story of a man from Beijing who migrates to New York and gets a job in a factory that is owned by a white American. The Chinese man ends up owning the factory and the American ends up without a job. According to Georgie it was the most popular serial in China. And this got me thinking.

In Morrison's day, missionaries, many of them women, from a dozen nations were fanning out across China, bringing Western ideas, beliefs and techniques to the interior for the first time. They brought churches, schools, hospitals, the very idea of social service. It can't be denied that some of them also brought arrogance and ignorance, and were sometimes forced to flee in front of rioting mobs.

In 1993 Western culture was being pumped into millions of households the length and breadth of China every single day, and they couldn't get enough of it.

Many of the towns and villages I had stayed in since leaving Chongqing didn't have running water; a lot of them didn't even have a local shop. The people were living with filth, farm animals and unmade roads. Yet every room of every dusty, down-at-heel truck-drivers' doss house I stayed in the entire time I was in China had a television. Maybe only a black and white television, maybe only a television that got one snowy channel for an hour or two a day while the electricity was on, but they all had it.

And the great thing about television is that it makes you want things.

The next day I was up and about and poking around the back lanes of Zhaotong, through shops and stalls stuffed with tea, tobacco and traditional

medicine, all roots and powders and strange curly things, and the day after I was
ready to start travelling the last section to Kunming.

Morrison rode the distance from Zhaotong to Kiangti — about 70 kilometres
(40 miles) — on his first day out. The best I could manage was a day and a half,
and I was hitchhiking.

But I couldn't help thinking that wherever Morrison walked, his porters walked
too. The difference was that these men, by his own description, were underfed,
barefoot illiterates. They also, of course, had to carry the luggage. When they got to
Dashuijing, a healthy 40 or so kilometres (25 miles) from Zhaotong, and the porters
had already arranged accommodation for the night, Morrison caught up with them
on his horse and insisted that they march on until after dark down a dangerous
descent to a small inn near the village of Kiangti. I, for one, couldn't see what the
hurry was.

* * *

For a few days I travelled along the upland that centres on Zhaotong. The country
is bare and exposed, a land of lonely farmhouses and dusty winds and grey gravelly
riverbeds scouring their way down from ranges even more remote, with pockets
and crevices where villages and towns shelter beneath grand, empty bluffs. Every
day or two I would hitchhike from one town to the next, jouncing along the scarred
roads in truck cabs foggy with the fumes of cheap cigarettes, chatting with drivers
whose Mandarin was as thickly accented as mine.

The towns were odd, hybrid specimens, where the blankness of modern
Chinese architecture seemed to have fought itself to a stalemate with the
mudbrick compounds, their battered wooden doors bright with peeling paper
prints of guardian deities. At the centre there was usually a town square of
recent design, where little stalls sold fiery rice liquor and crumbly biscuits and
rough, bloody hunks of pork by day, and by night video parlours showed
Hong Kong gangster movies, or tinny karaoke sets wailed full bore, piercing the
thin walls of the truckstops as I sat and wrote beneath paper-lined ceilings crusted
with fly spots.

I drank tea with farmers, simple broad-faced people with raw hands. I had
polite conversations with high school teachers, keen to practise their English. And
I got midnight visits from policemen and Party officials, who would ask with
semaphore and phrasebooks what I was doing in their town; they looked bemused
and bewildered when I tried to explain, and would peer, uncomprehending,
through my passport and then say, 'Welcome to China,' and wander off and leave
me to it.

When I wanted to order a meal, I would walk into the kitchen of whatever
restaurant I was in and point to whatever I fancied. This was usually tofu, or

aubergine, or cauliflower, as I fought a desperate rearguard action to stay vegetarian in the face of one of the most determinedly carnivorous societies in the world. Ten minutes later, I would be presented with a dish of tofu or aubergine or cauliflower, stir-fried in pig fat.

I gorged on sweet juicy mandarins at 1 yuan (20 Australian cents) a kilo. Crowds of children followed me up village lanes, shouting, 'How do you do!' and collapsing into giggles. The sun shone from dawn to dusk. I got a shower, I suppose, about once a week. I was filthy, furry and happy.

Then the road tilts down, and the land smooths to a rolling quilt of green and red, of autumn trees and pony carts and potato fields. The mountains become ridges of faded orange off in the distance with rice fields lapping at their base, and a railway appears, and then the highway turns into a headache of trucks and diesel and blaring horns as it approaches the city.

CHAPTER SEVEN

THE PAGODAS AND LOFTY TEMPLES OF THE FAMOUS CITY

Kunming

When he got to Kunming — Yunnan City, as it was called then — Morrison met Jensen, the Danish superintendent of telegraphs, and spent a week with him. 'It was a pleasant change from silence to speech, from Chinese discomfort to European civilisation. Chinese fare one evening,' he wrote, 'pork, rice, tea, and beans; and the next, chicken and the famed Shuenwei ham, mutton and green peas and red currant jelly, pancakes and aboriginal Yunnan cheese, claret, champagne, port, and cordial Medoc.'

'The pagoda of Yunnan City'

Europuropean 'civilisation' is available in Kunming today in the form of Liu's Café. I'd been reading the menu for a couple of minutes before I realised there was something odd going on — I was actually *reading* the menu. Even stranger, it spoke of items like muesli and yoghurt, buttered toast and French fries — the same fare that appears on identical dog-eared menus across Asia from Kuta Beach to Kashgar, in every place where half a dozen Western backpackers have ever stopped to wash their socks and dream dreams of the sixties. I descended on a couple of unsuspecting Danes dressed in a fetching mixture of Jimi Hendrix and Polartec and unloaded a couple of months of accumulated verbal diarrhoea through mouthfuls of banana pancake.

Modern Kunming seemed to be studded with high-rise buildings surmounted by revolving restaurants — or at least things that were meant to *resemble* revolving restaurants. There were also all the familiar features of the late twentieth-century Chinese city: dust, concrete, limousines, taxis, crowds, construction sites. But Kunming was different, too. The megacities of central China all have a haggard, careworn look to them. But Kunming had a youth and freshness that made me optimistic: there was less pollution, more sunshine, even trees in the streets.

It was time to do a bit more detective work. Because Kunming was Jensen's base, a lot of the photos in Morrison's book, as well as some extra pictures I'd dug out of the Morrison Collection at the Mitchell Library, were taken there. Like many a nineteenth-century photographer fascinated by the antiquities and physical trappings of a foreign culture, Jensen had concentrated on the monuments, the temples, the grand architecture, the cityscapes. Now all I had to do was go and find them.

From the bookshop in one of the turreted monoliths I bought two maps of Kunming, a guidebook to Kunming and a guidebook to Yunnan. I then sat down with these, a cup of tea, Morrison's description, Jensen's photographs and a map of Kunming that had been drawn, by the looks of it, in World War II. This had been given to me by Charles, a native of the city who now lives in Melbourne and who had very kindly volunteered all kinds of information when I had interviewed him before leaving Australia. Over the next couple of hours I assembled the clues, refilling my teacup from a thermos as I went.

Kunming, like just about every other town in China, used to have a city wall. 'This is one of the most massive walls in a country of walled cities. It is built of brick and stone over a body of earth thirty feet thick; it is of imposing height, and wide enough for a carriage drive,' Morrison wrote. There were a couple of photos of it, too. One was of the east gate of the city — the gate through which Morrison rode when he arrived. By matching my old map, which had the wall marked on it, to the new ones, I was soon able to plot the route of the wall and the position of the gate in relation to modern Kunming. Mostly the wall followed an inner ring road that now surrounds the centre of the city. I picked up my camera bag and headed down there.

At the site of the gate, which had been an imposing, triple-roofed structure of tiles and brick, easily the height of a modern three-storey building, with delicately painted woodwork above a crenellated stone wall that looked like something out of a Robin Hood film, and intricately carved stone lions guarding the entrance from either side, there stood nothing. Nothing at all.

The east gate of Yunnan City had been replaced by a traffic intersection. Bicycles and vans and cars whizzed past along the six-lane road. On one side were some commercial buildings. On the other, hessian-clad scaffolding, screaming tools and cement mixers surrounded ... a new high rise. I got a few shots and started walking along the route where the city wall once lay. I followed the three-lane road around in a big semicircle, south, then west, then north-west ...

I walked for three hours. Of that huge city wall, 7 kilometres (4 miles) round and 10 metres (33 feet) high, not one brick remained.

Somewhere in the north of the city, I got lost. Dusk was falling and I'd wandered off the ring road and into a maze of narrow alleys.

'Where do you want to go?' said a voice.

I looked up from my map. He must have been about seventy, with a gentle, bird-like face. He looked a little the worse for wear.

'Which place are you looking for? Perhaps I can help you.'

He was in a faded blue Mao suit, cap and all. He had a strong growth of white whiskers and his teeth were a brown mess of decay. He was walking a heavy black bicycle.

'I'm looking for the city wall. Is any of it left? Do you know where I can find it?'

'Oh.' He smiled. 'That is gone, long ago. It used to be along here, but it was taken away after the war. It was in the way of the traffic.'

'Do you remember it?'

'Oh yes. I have lived in Kunming all my life. My name is Chou.' We shook hands. 'During the war I learned English from the American airmen who stayed here. I was fifteen or sixteen then. I was working in a department store. They used to come into my shop often to buy things. I learned English by talking to them.'

I remembered reading about these American pilots. They had come as a volunteer unit, mercenaries really, before Pearl Harbor, when the Americans were looking for discreet ways to slow down the Japanese. The Chinese had little air power and were powerless to stop, among other things, the relentless bombing of Chongqing. So the Americans had lent them planes and pilots, and the unit had been based in Kunming. Later the American fliers became the only link to the outside world when the Japanese took Indochina and Burma and slammed China's back door shut in 1942. The Americans freighted in supplies from small airfields in eastern India across the 'hump' — the towering spur of mountains that runs from northern Burma up to the Himalayas — often having to fly at twice their normal altitude in turbulence that could warp the fuselage of a C-46 in mid-air. In 1944 three people died for every 100 tons of supplies flown in over the hump. Others got rich.

The war transformed Kunming from a sleepy provincial centre into a busy cosmopolitan city as it did Chongqing, only more so. Three universities and countless refugees relocated here after fleeing the Japanese, and roads took the place of the ancient footpaths linking it to Burma and other parts of China. The scholars brought their erudition, the refugees brought their bundles of belongings, and the Americans, predictably enough, brought money, jazz, prostitutes and a thriving black market.

'I collect foreign money,' Chou was saying. 'I like to help tourists. Many of them give me foreign currency. Once I held an exhibition of my collection, in a park near here.' He showed me some photos of his exhibition. 'Chinese people are very interested in money,' he told me. It crossed my mind that Chou might have got more out of those American pilots than just English lessons.

'Do you have any Australian money you could give me?' he asked.

I seemed to remember a few odd coins swimming around the bottom of my backpack. 'Yes,' I said, 'but they're in my hotel. Can you meet me there tomorrow? You might be able to help me with something.'

I went back to Liu's, ordered a pizza and a chocolate pancake and a bottle of Kunming beer, and unloaded another deluge of linguistic effluent on another hapless backpacker.

I met Chou in the lobby of the hotel the next morning at eleven. I'd dug out a $1 and a $2 coin, which I presented to him. He was ecstatic with this haul: he liked the kangaroos on the $1 and the nuggetty goldness of the $2.

'I need to find some places in Kunming. Can you help me?' I asked. I pulled out Morrison and some extra photos I'd found in the Morrison Collection.

There were a couple of temples which he pointed out straightaway on the map, and a view across rooftops that could have been taken anywhere in the city. There was also a picture of a pagoda, which the caption said was 250 feet (76 metres) high. 'There are two pagodas like this,' said Chou. 'They are called the West Pagoda and the East Pagoda. They are near here. I can take you there.'

There was one other picture. It was captioned 'The Mission of the Missions Etrangères de Paris, Yunnan City', and it showed a slightly eccentric-looking nineteenth-century building of European design which, according to Morrison, had been a college where Chinese students were trained for the priesthood. Two storeys high, with an arched balcony and a cross at the apex of the facade, it looked like Spanish colonial gone wrong. Chou didn't recognise it.

I looked it up in the book. According to Morrison, the mission was 10 miles (16 kilometres) outside the city, and was 'known throughout the Province as Jinmaasuh [now Jinmasu]'.

'Have you heard of Jinmasu?' I asked Chou.

'Yes, I know it. I can take you there. We can get there by bicycle.'

We walked to a shop near by that Chou knew about and I hired a bicycle identical to his. It was one of those heavy black indestructible one-gear workhorses that Chinese factories churn out by the million. Where the Chinese economy would be today without them is anybody's guess. I've seen them used to carry everything from live pigs to bags of cement to buckets of human manure on its way to the fields where it is used for fertiliser. But mostly they are just used by millions upon millions upon millions of people every day to commute. Just pushing the weight of the frame was nearly enough to do me in that afternoon.

The city thinned and the buildings gradually became interspersed with little patchwork plots of market garden. We crossed the Kunming–Hanoi railway line, and rode past a large development of what Chou told me were luxury apartments for the nouveaux riches of Kunming. As we rode, he told me some more about his life.

'After the war I started my own business,' he said. 'I became a merchant, dealing in medicines. In 1950 I went to Burma to buy some medicines. I went by truck all the way to Rangoon, down the Burma Road. It was a very rough trip. It took me one week. By the road there were many trucks and tanks, abandoned when they broke down or ran out of fuel.'

I tried to picture Rangoon in 1950. It brought to mind scratchy black-and-white newsreel, white suits and sola topis, sacks of rice and palm trees, little old cars with running boards, gin and tonics and slow wobbly ceiling fans. All of which is not, in fact, too far removed from the Rangoon of 1994.

'Then the government took over my business. So I learned Russian. At that time our country was very close to Russia. For some years I was a Russian teacher. Then in 1960 China had a fight with Russia. After that we didn't need Russian teachers any more. So I went to work in a factory. I worked at the factory until I retired a few years ago.'

I wondered how he'd fared during the anti-rightist campaigns of the fifties and the Cultural Revolution, when anyone with the slightest connection to the capitalists and landlords and exploiters of the old regime was liable to be persecuted, humiliated and beaten, sometimes to death.

'What was it like in the sixties?' I prodded, as gently as I could.

A cloud passed over his face. 'You mean, the Cultural Revolution?'

'Yes, I suppose so.'

'Why do all you foreigners always ask about that? It was a bad time, of course.

But it was long ago. Of course I suffered. Everybody suffered. Now I prefer to forget it.'

'I'm sorry,' I said, and we were silent for a while.

We reached Jinmasu, which is now an outer suburb of Kunming. Chou showed the picture of the mission to some locals and asked them if they knew where it was. Eventually someone directed us to the local school, which turned out to be a concrete compound surrounded by brick buildings. Dozens of ten-year-old boys, all with crew cuts, were playing basketball, but abandoned their game to surround us while Chou spoke to the teachers.

'This is the place where that building was,' he said. 'Over there you can see the Jinma temple. It is a very old temple. It was a famous place in this area. *Jinma* means "golden horse". That means that once there would have been a statue of a golden horse here.'

I looked where he was pointing. There was indeed an old building in the corner, looking a little dilapidated. I peered inside and saw a pile of small chairs and desks, broken and dusty: the Golden Horse Temple had become a school storeroom. The mission building, if indeed it had stood here, had disappeared without a trace. I took a few pictures while the teachers and students looked on, bemused. Then something else caught my eye. Sticking up behind the roof of the temple, at a somewhat drunken angle, was the top of a pagoda, in the same distinctive style as the pagodas in Morrison's book. I took the book out again and leafed through it.

Opposite page 118 I found it. The caption just said 'Pagoda by the wayside, Western China'. I had looked at it 100 times, and each time I'd thought, I don't have a hope in hell of finding that. In the photo, the pagoda was surrounded by trees, with a mud brick building to one side, and some boys sitting at the base looking at the camera. Even in Jensen's time, it had looked old.

The top half of the pagoda that I saw sticking up behind the school buildings looked very, very similar. We left the compound and followed the wall round to the back to have a closer look, eventually arriving at a building that turned out to be the headquarters of the local municipal corporation. Some office workers were having lunch under a tree. Behind the tree was a little courtyard and at the back of the courtyard stood the pagoda, leaning like the tower of Pisa with weeds growing out of its roof, exactly as they had been in Morrison's time. I looked at the photo again. It was either the same one, or so similar you couldn't tell the difference. I couldn't believe it — it was like locating a tenth-century shipwreck at the bottom of an urban ocean. And the thought that it had just been sitting here half-forgotten these 100 years while the world turned itself upside-down around it, and would probably sit here till everyone alive today, including me, is dead and the world has turned itself upside-down a few more times, sent a shiver up my spine.

中国

'Pagoda by the wayside, Western China'

Pagoda at Jinmasu, Kunming

Top and bottom: *The Muslim quarter, Kunming*

Noodle-making in the Muslim quarter

中国

'Soldiers on the city wall of Yunnan City'

Soldiers on Beijing Road, Kunming

'The big east gate of Yunnan City'

Site of the former east gate of Kunming

'View in Yunnan City'

View in Kunming

'Temple in Yunnan City'

Daguanlou Grand Mansion, Kunming

Old man practising tai chi, Kunming

Yuantong Temple, Kunming

Groom greeting guests at a wedding reception, Kunming

Chou was talking to the office workers. I went over and showed them the picture. '*Yi bai nian qian*' was all I could say by way of explanation — '100 years ago'. They pointed at it and talked about it to each other and had a good laugh. I couldn't understand what they were saying, but I think I could guess.

'Who is this overgrown foreigner and why has he come here, and why is he here with this old man who can speak his language, and what is that book he keeps looking at? And why in the name of Confucius and Buddha and Mao and Deng is there a picture of our pagoda in it?'

I asked them to stand under the pagoda while I photographed it. This brought on a fresh round of laughter. Then Chou and I rode back towards the city. I felt like a golfer who's just got a hole-in-one.

Chou took me past the textiles factory where he had worked most of his life. 'I had a very good job there,' he said. 'I used to procure supplies for the factory. I used to ride around the town on my bicycle all day, going to shops and other factories to order things. Now my wife and I are retired. We both worked in the same factory. We still live in the apartment provided by the factory. We pay 5 yuan a month for rent. My pension is ninety per cent of what I used to earn in the factory.'

China is a billion stories like Mr Chou's. His, it seems, is having a happy ending.

We rode on to the West Pagoda. It wasn't the one in Morrison's book and it wasn't 250 feet high, but I didn't care. It was built in AD 859, according to the guidebook, and it was as solid as a pre-war Buick. Surrounding it was a little park where pensioners sat and played mah-jong and Chinese chess and smoked and drank tea and chewed the fat in the warm sun.

It was getting late. We rode back into town, dodging the rush hour chaos in the fading light. I was hot and bothered and sweating. Chou just sailed on steadily. In quick succession he showed me a Catholic church dating from the 1930s, a lavish and spanking new Protestant church, and the Muslim quarter.

Kunming was made the capital of Yunnan by Kublai Khan after he subjugated the province. Some years later Marco Polo visited the city, which he called Yachi, on a tour of inspection for the Khan. 'The inhabitants are of several sorts,' he wrote. 'There are some who worship Mahomet, some idolaters and a few Nestorian Christians.' That was in 1278 or thereabouts. In 1994 the Mongols have gone, the Christians have left and come back, and the Muslims have been there all along.

A sickly stench rose from a series of stalls that lined the main street of the quarter for a kilometre or so; each consisted of a wooden frame hung with dozens of half-dried slabs of lamb, slowly curing in the smog and dust as customers ambled by and made their choice. Men with white caps and pointy beards sold kebabs which had been sprinkled with chilli and salt before being barbecued on beds of hot coals. There were signs in what looked like Arabic script and pictures of Mecca and a lot of women who didn't appear too bothered about covering their heads.

When we got back to the bike shop, I tried to give Chou some money, to thank him, but he wouldn't accept it. However, I noticed that he stayed behind at the shop when I went back to my hotel — taking a cut of my rental, I guessed.

The next day I rode out to Daguan Park on the western side of the city, where Chou had told me I would find one of the temples Jensen had photographed. It was a haven of willows, lakes and lotus, dating back to the seventeenth century. There, by the lake, stood the Daguanlou Grand Mansion, identical to the picture I had found in the Morrison Collection identified only as 'Temple in Yunnan City'. Built in 1690, its colours and proportions were a study in grace. On either side of the entrance, a poem and commentary were inscribed. The commentary lists a succession of conquerors from the north:

> Several thousand years of history in my heart,
> Wine cools in the pot.
> Heaving sighs for absent heroes, I think:
> The Han built tall ships
> The Tang set up iron pillars
> The Song wielded jade axes
> The Yuan rode with leather saddlebags
> The exploits of their heroes were glorious,
> Inspired by the spirit to move mountains,
> They respected the pearl curtains and painted ridge pole
> Through endless evening rains and morning clouds.
> But the stone tablets recording their exploits
> Are cracked and broken, gone to ashes, scattered;
> All they achieved, a double line of autumn geese,
> A frosted pillow.

The author of the original poem, Sun Ranweng, a reclusive scholar, is reputed to have been a Ming loyalist who never accepted the Qing takeover. If he came back today, he might add another lot to the list: the threadbare Red Army dodging its way past Kunming in 1935, halfway to the refuge of the empty hills of Shaanxi where it would arrive six months later one-tenth the size it started out, having crossed eighteen mountain ranges, twenty-four rivers and twelve provinces during its 8,000-kilometre (4,971-mile) Long March. And then returning in 1949, the undisputed ruler of China, to drive what was left of the local Guomindang army into the jungles of Burma.

Later I found myself back at the mosque in the Muslim quarter — an open prayer room beneath a classical curved roof — listening as the mullah warbled Friday prayers to hundreds of believers. Welcoming faces beckoned me to join in, and afterwards, an enthusiastic young man came up to me and started telling me about the mosque.

'Are you a Muslim?' he asked me.

'Well, I'm ... um, a Christian.'

'Oh, so that means we believe in the same God. Not like these people,' and he waved dismissively at some Han in the alleyway outside.

'Well, actually, I er ...' I've been in this situation a thousand times in India, and have found that non-belief is as unfathomable to the devotee as faith is to the atheist.

Then Chou appeared, still in his washed-out blue suit. He had a couple more coins with him. He couldn't read the writing on them and, thinking it might be Arabic, had come here to find out where they came from. I looked at them, and identified one of them as Sri Lankan. My Muslim friend told him that the other one was from Tunisia. Where Chou had got them from, I cannot conceive.

CHAPTER EIGHT

'From Yunnan City to Bhamo on the Irrawaddy, in British Burma, is a difficult journey of thirty-three stages over a mountainous road which can never by any human possibility be made available for other traffic than caravans of horses or coolies on foot.'

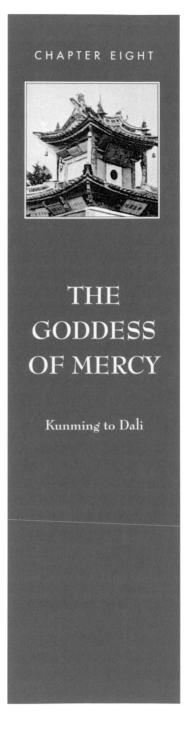

THE GODDESS OF MERCY

Kunming to Dali

'Memorial in the Temple of the Goddess of Mercy, near Tali-fu'

On this point the famous correspondent-to-be was completely wrong. When eastern China fell to the Japanese, the old mule trail to Burma suddenly became an essential link to the outside world. With the kind of purpose that takes hold when you're scared out of your wits, the Guomindang threw down a highway stretching nearly 1,000 kilometres (620 miles) over this supposedly impenetrable barrier in just two years. The famous Burma Road was built by 200,000 peasants drafted in waves from nearby villages as the road progressed, using bamboo baskets, farm tools and primitive rollers carved out of limestone cliffs with hammers and chisels. At the border it linked up with a road that the British had built up from Lashio in the Burmese hills, where a train line connected it to Rangoon and the rest of the world. It didn't, in the end, make all that much difference to the war effort.

But it made a big difference to me. Morrison, setting out from Kunming with the same three porters and a new pony, took three days to get to a town called Lufeng, which he called Lu-feng-hsien. It took me three hours. When we got there, I jumped off the bus, heaved my pack on to a horse cart and rode the remaining couple of kilometres to the centre. Lufeng is most famous these days for its fossilised dinosaurs; there is a statue of several of them in a traffic roundabout in the middle of town.

I was looking for another kind of relic, a bridge this time. There wasn't a photo of it in Morrison's book and, as it turned out, there didn't need to be. I asked a woman who was tending a vegetable patch where I might find an old bridge. I got some eager nods, and a small boy was detailed to show me the way. Five minutes later, I was there.

> The finest stone bridge I have seen in Western China, and one that would arrest attention in any country in the world, is at this town. It crosses the wide bed of a stream that in winter is insignificant, but which grows in volume in the rains of summer to a broad and powerful river. It is a bridge of seven beautiful arches; it is 12 yards broad and 150 yards long, of perfect simplicity and symmetry, with massive piers, all built of dressed masonry and destined to survive the lapse of centuries. Triumphal archways with memorial tablets and pedestals of carved lions are befitting portals to a really noble work.

There's not much I can add. There it was, triumphal archways, carved lions and all. It had survived the lapse of one century, and was looking good for another couple. I could almost see Morrison wandering about with his tape measure while his men rolled their eyes and grabbed the chance for a quick smoke. Whatever his shortcomings, the man certainly had a gift for precisely detailed description.

Xingxiu bridge, Lufeng

Morrison said something else about the area that interested me. Every town he passed through lay in ruins, he wrote, and the countryside was practically deserted. This was the legacy of the great Muslim rebellion of 1855–73.

The rebellion erupted as Yunnan's large Muslim population came into conflict over land ownership and mining rights with Han migrants who were then streaming in from poverty-stricken neighbouring provinces. The Muslims jacked up, declared their own kingdom, and held on to it for eighteen years. When the Manchus finally managed to put the rebellion down, helped out by artillery supplied by the French, the carnage was indescribable. According to one source, Yunnan's Muslim population today — about 200,000 — is one-tenth what it was 100 years ago. The official line on the rebellion these days is that it was a glorious peasant rising, a forerunner to the communist revolution.

South of Kunming, towards the Vietnamese border, there is a town called Shadian. During the Muslim rebellion it was an important centre for the manufacture of armaments. According to the American academic Dru C. Gladney, in 1968, at the height of the Cultural Revolution, when it was open season on any type of religious observance, a battle broke out between 'leftist' and 'revisionist' Muslims of Shadian. When the army came in to restore order, they attacked the religious leaders, forcing them to eat pork and imitate pigs. Pork bones were thrown into wells.

A few years later, as the Cultural Revolution wound down, some of the 'revisionists' asked permission to reopen their mosque. It was refused. The rival groups clashed again, this time leaving several people dead.

At three in the morning on 29th July 1975 several regiments of the People's Liberation Army entered Shadian to take control of the situation. According to the witnesses interviewed by Gladney, the soldiers were supported by artillery and MiG jets armed with rockets. The fighting, which soon spread to surrounding villages, lasted a week. When the smoke cleared, more than 1,600 Muslims lay dead and the entire township of Shadian, 4,400 houses in all, had been razed to the ground.

In 1979, following the fall of the Gang of Four, the village was rebuilt, the villagers were compensated and an apology was made.

I remembered asking Georgie, my friend in Zhaotong, about the local Muslims.

'We call these people the Hui,' he had said. 'They have a reputation for being smugglers. They live all over China, so they have good networks. Also, they have contact with Muslims in other countries. Now Yunnan has a big problem with drug smuggling, and most of the smugglers are Hui. They don't care about the law — you see, they do not regard themselves as Chinese. Many of them believe in those leaders from Iran. Actually, we have a saying about these people — that they are ignorant but brave.'

I'd decided to do a bit of fishing. 'And what do you think of the Yi people?' I asked, referring to Yunnan's biggest minority, hill-dwellers who are animist, Buddhist or Christian.

'Oh,' laughed Georgie, 'we say that these people are ignorant but not brave!'

For the last five years or so there have been regular reports of separatist demonstrations in Xinjiang, the enormous, largely Muslim province in China's far west that borders the newly independent republics of Central Asia.

'There is a fearlessness and independence of bearing in the Mohammedan, a militant carriage that distinguishes him from the Chinese unbeliever,' wrote Morrison. China has about fifteen million Muslims.

* * *

That night I pulled out my maps again. Another of Jensen's photos was coming up. This time it had been taken in a village; there was a mud brick house, a shed, a pack animal, some piles of wood, and a few villagers staring curiously at the foreigner with his contraption. Unlike the rest of Jensen's photos, it was an ordinary scene, a window into everyday life. Morrison identified it as '"The Eagle Nest Barrier" on the road between Yunnan and Tali', but the only clue to its whereabouts was that it was at a village called Ying-wu-kwan, 'midway between Shachiaokai and Pupêng', at an elevation of more than 8,000 feet (2,438 metres).

On my modern map of Yunnan, I found the towns of Shaqiao and Pupeng; they were further west along the highway. Then I went back to an older map which had the elevations marked in feet. Between the two towns there was a town called Tianshentang at 8,100 feet (2,469 metres). Next morning, I rolled out of bed, splashed some water on my face, and bought a ticket for the bus.

Straight out of Lufeng the bus ducked into a narrow valley where steep wooded ridges closed in the highway. The road was dirt again, and houses were few and far between. We charged around bends and down tunnels and eventually the country opened out again and there were rolling hills etched with terraces. The day waxed warmer, the dust flew about, and the pattern repeated itself, gentle hills alternating with claustrophobic ravines. Every once in a while I caught sight of the concrete struts and girders of a new railway line, clawing its way over the mountains in the direction of Burma, along with me, my backpack and the juggernaut of Han civilisation. Over the range to our right lay the Yangtze, here making a great bend to the south, which I'd been following in parallel since leaving Sichuan six weeks before. Still 2,000 kilometres (1,243 miles) from its source, it is in this stretch known as the Jinsha Jiang — the River of Golden Sand — a fast stream tumbling through the mountains.

We began to climb the main range. The forest closed in again, the air cooled, the engine steamed. Then we were suddenly descending and there was a small reservoir and a few fields. A line of wood and mud buildings straggled along the road for a few hundred metres. This had to be it. I asked the driver to stop, hauled my pack off the cover of the panting engine, and began the usual search for a room.

Tianshentang was definitely a one-hotel town, and the local motor inn didn't take much tracking down. I walked through a kitchen that was thick with soot and dirt. Pigs were grovelling in the yard and a little boy was pelting a little girl with mud. I took a room with a ceiling so low I couldn't stand up straight, dropped the dead weight of my pack and got out again. The afternoon was pressing on.

There was a market in the main square. Women of a minority I didn't recognise were bargaining for clothes; they all wore richly embroidered blue tunics, green Mao caps and shaggy brown goatskins across their backs. A few of them were having a picnic on the grass before heading home on trailers drawn by putt-putting outboard motors steered with handlebars. The menfolk were intently playing pool on a collection of outdoor tables whose surfaces brought to mind the contours of the Yunnan–Guizhou Tableland.

I asked the way to Yingwuguan, the 'Eagle Nest Barrier' featured in Jensen's picture, and was pointed up the hill in the direction my bus had come from. I started walking and was soon in the forest. It was eucalyptus, which always reminds me of home, less because of how it looks than by its distinctive smell. I didn't get a chance to get too sentimental, though. A constant stream of trucks was passing on the highway, leaving a lingering pall of diesel exhaust hanging in the air.

I climbed for forty minutes or so. There was a petrol station at the top, and a few more houses. I asked again, and was told to go about another kilometre in the same direction.

When I finally got there, the sun was lowering on the little settlement of Yingwuguan, a hamlet of about eight houses which is so small it wasn't marked on any of the maps I had. The mudbrick houses, each with a porch, a wooden frame supported by pillars, a loft and a curved, tiled roof, were identical to the one in the photo. There was even a new one being built, to exactly the same pattern. There were pigs in wooden cages and chickens and piles of chopped wood and farm tools lying around.

I looked around and found a house that looked very much like the one in the original picture. To one side, now obscured by a more recent building, I could even see the old shed. I took some photos but the light was getting low. Then a man came out of the house, probably a direct descendant of one of the people in Jensen's picture. He was about forty, with a moustache that consisted of a couple of dozen hardy black hairs, and he looked a little surprised to see me. I showed him the photograph and tried to explain that it was of his house; but what he made of it I don't really know. He offered me a cigarette and invited me in and gave me a cup of tea and a handful of sunflower seeds to nibble. He asked me which places I'd been to in China, and I ran through the list, beginning at Shanghai and ending at Yingwuguan. Suddenly Shanghai seemed a very long way away.

His wife was sitting on the lounge sewing, and she nodded at me and smiled. My host had unbuttoned his jacket. Underneath it he had on a white T-shirt that featured a cartoon character with yellow skin. It said, 'I'm BART SIMPSON. WHO THE HELL ARE YOU?' The TV was on, but the reception was fuzzy and you could hardly make out the picture.

I walked back down to Tianshentang and accepted a challenge to a game of pool in the last of the daylight. I'm no Paul Newman at the best of times, and the uneven surface and the fading light and the fact that there was a crowd packed three deep around the table to watch the foreigner play didn't add much to my game. By the time we finished, an hour and a half later, the stars were bright in the sky.

Next morning I walked back up to Yingwuguan to get the picture. Except for electricity and the highway and polyester clothes all round, it seemed that life hadn't changed in this tiny village in 100 years. Or had it? Perhaps the changes had occurred in a way that the camera couldn't capture. No one was starving; no one was addicted to opium; no one had bound feet; no one was in hock to a grasping landlord. Along with temples and pagodas and city walls, quite a few things had been trashed in the last 100 years which had well and truly had it coming.

I walked back down to Tianshentang and had my standard breakfast, a bowl of noodles with eggs and vegetables. Then I thumbed a lift to Dali.

* * *

Dali, or Tali as it was spelled by Westerners in Morrison's time, has been slipping in and out of Chinese hands for centuries. The present city dates back to the Ming dynasty, but as recently as the 1870s it was the capital of the short-lived Muslim kingdom of Du Wenxiu. Strategically located, Dali was the point where caravans from Sichuan, Burma, Tibet and India would converge, trade and reassemble for the return or onward journey; Morrison noted a couple of enormous caravanserais here. It is also, as every writer who has ever visited it notes, gloriously beautiful.

Nowadays Dali is full of Chinese tourists who come here to cruise on its lake, take pictures of each other standing in front of its pagodas, and buy carvings made from its famous marble. It is also full of young Westerners who climb its mountain, take pictures of its pagodas without standing in front of them, buy souvenirs that are a bit more suited to air travel, and smoke the marijuana that grows wild in the streets. There are also Burmese, Tibetans, Thais, Muslims, and half a dozen other

Hard Rock Café, Dali

races I couldn't even identify. Numbers of women were wearing mulberry tunics over jeans or blue work pants; these are the Bai, prominent among the minorities, descendants of the people who ran the place for five centuries before Kublai Khan's army arrived.

There were two photos I had to find. One was of Cangshan. As this mountain is 4,100 metres (13,451 feet) high and dominates the city from every angle, it wasn't too difficult to track down. It was the first thing I saw when I looked out of my hotel window in the morning, the copper clouds of dawn brushing its hefty, snow-dusted flanks. The other photo was of the temple to the Goddess of Mercy, beyond the city wall on the highway, a place for the travellers and traders and caravan masters who once streamed through the city to pray for good luck on their journeys. It, too, was just as Morrison left it.

In the afternoon I climbed some of the way up the mountain to get a view of the valley. I was looking for the Phoenix Eye Cave. Morrison had tried to climb up there, but his energy had given out halfway. Here, then, was my big chance: I might, for once, be able to beat him to something, no matter how trivial. It didn't matter to me that he'd just walked or ridden a pony all the way from Kunming and had a perfect right to be exhausted. I had to outdo him in at least *something*.

> Tali is situated on the undulating ground that shelves gently from the base of snow-clad mountains down to the lake. The lower slopes of the mountains, above the town, are covered with myriads of grave-mounds, which in the distance are scarcely distinguishable from the granite blocks around them Creeks and rills of running water spring from the melting of the snows far up the mountain, run among the grave-mounds, and are then trained into the town. The Chinese residents thus enjoy the privilege of drinking a diluted solution of their ancestors.

From my map I deduced that the graveyard must be on the way to the cave, so I stumbled up through it, stopping for tea at a Buddhist monastery nestling in the pines, and talking for an hour with an English actress who happened to be having tea there too. Some old men and women were laboriously brushing prayers on to slips of yellow paper, which they would then burn in front of an altar. Below us stretched the green, grey and gold checks of the fields, the 40-kilometre (25-mile) turquoise sheen of Erhai Lake, the rusty hills behind and the walled city in front. If the view had been a meal it would have been smoked salmon, salad and champagne — good for the mind, good for the body and good for the soul.

I spent the afternoon walking along a stone pathway that cut through the cool forest along the contour of the mountain, the valley constantly in view to my left. I never did find the cave.

I passed the evening at the Café de Jack, a spot favoured by the Western contingent. Jack was an affable Muslim who drank like a small whale and probably indulged in one or two other vices as well, to judge by the perpetual smile on his face. He had picked up his very good English from speaking to backpackers, and his accent and idioms were liable to jump from New Zealand to New York to Sweden to Israel in the space of a sentence. Jack kept a fridge full of cold beer and served a chocolate cake and ice cream that were better than sex. Or at least the best available alternative.

Never a fast learner, I waded once more into the Chinese brandy, this time in the company of a Greek photographer, a Boston taxi driver, two lads from Brisbane and a couple of girls from Bavaria. As I teetered back to the hotel at three a.m., the clouds had peeled back in high cottonwool bunches to the north and south to reveal an indigo banner spattered with stars, from Cangshan in the west to Erhai Lake in the east. It was Christmas morning.

* * *

When Morrison did his walk, he certainly wasn't the first Westerner to pass this way. The same Treaty of Tientsin that had given foreigners such as Morrison the right to travel in the interior with full protection from local authorities — a treaty negotiated in 1860 while the British and French had their guns trained on Peking — had also given Christian missionaries the right to proselytise anywhere in China.

China was the last great untapped reservoir of lost souls, and the floodgates had opened. Before 1860 there were missionary establishments only in the five Treaty ports; by the turn of the century there were resident missionaries all over the country, toiling away in remote corners of every one of China's eighteen provinces. Morrison would never have made it across China without their help. Then, when he was safely out of China and their backs were turned, he sunk the knife in. 'During the time I was in China,' he wrote in *An Australian in China*, 'I met large numbers of missionaries of all classes, in many cities from Peking to Canton, and they unanimously expressed satisfaction at the progress they are making in China.'

> Expressed succinctly, their harvest may be described as amounting to a fraction more than two Chinamen per missionary per annum. If, however, the paid ordained and unordained native helpers be added to the number of missionaries, you find that the aggregate body converts nine-tenths of a Chinaman per worker per annum; but the missionaries deprecate their work being judged by statistics. There are 1,511 Protestant missionaries labouring in the Empire and, estimating their results from the statistics of previous years as published in the

> *Chinese Recorder*, we find that they gathered last year (1893)
> into the fold 3127 Chinese — not all of whom it is feared are
> genuine Christians — at a cost of £350,000, a sum equal to the
> combined incomes of the ten chief London hospitals.

In the last decade of the nineteenth century, missions representing the Daughters of Charity, the Canossian Sisters, the Société des Auxiliatrices des Ames de Purgatoire, the Carmelites, the Franciscans, the Dominicans, the Augustinians, the Lazarists, the Society of Servants of the Holy Ghost, the Congregation of the Immaculate Heart of Mary, the Seminary of Foreign Missions of Milan, the Society of the Divine Word, the Marist Brothers, the Salesians, the Jesuits, the Société des Missions Etrangères de Paris, the London Missionary Society, the (Dutch) Reformed Church in America, the Church Missionary Society, the Church of England Zenana Missionary Society, the American Baptists, the Gospel Baptist Mission, the Seventh Day Baptist Missionary Society, the (English) Baptist Missionary Society, the Basel German Evangelical Society, the Berlin Missionary Society for China, the Rhenish Missionary Society, the Methodist Episcopal Church of the Northern States, the Methodist Episcopal Church of the Southern States, the Methodist New Connexion, the English Methodist Free Church Mission, the Canadian Methodists, the Wesleyan Missionary Society, the American Presbyterians, the English Presbyterians, the Irish Presbyterians, the Presbyterian Church of Canada, the Reformed Presbyterian Church (Covenanter) in North America, the Cumberland Presbyterian Church, the British and Foreign Bible Society, the American Bible Society, the Pomeranian Mission Union for the Evangelization of China, the Society for the Propagation of the Gospel in Foreign Parts, the Evangelical Missionary Society of Paris, the China Inland Mission, the Church of Scotland, the United Free Church of Scotland, the China Congregational Society, the Friends Foreign Mission Association, the Ohio Yearly Meeting of Friends, the Disciples of Christ, the Christian and Missionary Alliance, the American Swedish Free Mission Society, the Swedish Evangelical Missionary Covenant of America, the Swedish Missionary Union, the Swedish Baptist Mission, the Norwegian Lutheran China Mission Association, the Free Church of Finland, the German Mission to Blind Females in China, the United Brethren of Christ, the Plymouth Brethren, the American Advent Mission Society, the YMCA, the YWCA and the Young People's Society for Christian Endeavor, were established.

I've never heard of half of these orders myself. What the Chinese made of it all, I can only wonder.

I fought off the waves of nausea and ignored the familiar brandy headache, struggled out of my warm bed and went down to the pile of grey stone on the main street that was the Dali Church of Christ. The service kicked off at ten. There were about thirty people there, and most of them looked to be past seventy, though there was a sprinkling of younger ones.

It started off with a rendition of 'Once in Royal David's City'. A plump, happy-looking old woman in thick glasses was playing a foot-pumped portable organ at the front as the wobbly old voices rose to the rafters. The words, of course, were in Chinese. This was followed by 'Silent Night'. Suddenly a wave of emotion came over me and I felt a long way from home. I forgot about all the crass consumerism that Christmas entails in the West and for a brief moment caught a glimpse of the magic it had brought when I was a child.

When the singing finally ground to a halt, an old man in a Mao cap got up and started to preach. Children were running around and playing in the aisles; people were gossiping to each other; and some of them were listening. Someone handed me an English Bible, which had been donated by an American church, and pointed out the reading. I looked through it, thinking that out here, among strangers and far from home, I might get some fresh insight into the familiar words. But all I saw was the same old stuff they'd tried unsuccessfully to drum into my head for five years at Canberra Grammar School.

Which somehow only made the scene around me all the more inspiring. Each of these people, no doubt, had endured ridicule and persecution, standing by their beliefs, though their only support came from half a world away.

We sang 'Silent Night' again, and a few other old favourites, and then everyone started to file out. We'd been in there for two hours, and it was a relief to emerge into the warm sun. I was invited to join the congregation for Christmas dinner in a nearby restaurant. I sat between Mrs Wu, the wife of the deacon who had taken the service, and a younger woman. Both of them spoke a little English. Plate after plate arrived from the kitchen, each one piled high with a different kind of meat. Out of politeness, people kept picking pieces up with their chopsticks and placing them on my plate. None of this did anything to help my hangover.

'Are your parents Christian?' I asked the younger woman who, as it turned out, was a nurse.

'My father is a doctor. My mother is cadre.'

'A cadre in the Communist Party?'

'No. I am League member.'

'What league?'

'Yes.'

'But are your mother and father Christian?' I tried again.

'Yes, Christian. We believe in dog.'

'You mean, you believe in God? A dog is an animal.'

'Yes, my family have dog. Pet dog.'

I turned to Mrs Wu. She told me that the church had been built by the China Inland Mission, the biggest of the Protestant missions, in 1913. The mission had first arrived in Dali in 1881. In 1941 they had built a hospital, which still existed though it was now run by the government. The missionaries had all had to leave in 1951.

'And what about the Catholics? Did they have a mission here?'

'Yes,' said Mrs Wu. 'There is a church.'

'How many Catholics are there in Dali?'

'I don't know. Maybe ten. I don't believe what they believe. These people think Mary was God. I think Mary was good girl. But there is only one God. You?'

'Sure.'

So there it was. Seventy years of missionary work, leaving a total of forty mostly moribund Christians. As Morrison points out with grinding regularity, the missionaries, for all their dedication, got virtually no converts.

But the missionaries were energetic healers and educators, building schools and hospitals, teaching European languages and spreading ideas that would one day fire a revolution. Ironically, one of the ideas that was acquired was godless communism, which would boot the missionaries out unceremoniously as soon as it was in a position to do so. As Mrs Wu had said, the Dali hospital was founded by the mission, then taken over by the government after Liberation. Today its much-expanded concrete bulk dwarfs the little grey stone church in front of it.

That afternoon I enjoyed something I'd almost forgotten about: a long sweet dreamless snooze in the sun. When I got to Jack's that evening for my second Christmas dinner, the air was hazy and Led Zeppelin was thumping from the stereo. I can't say I ever expected in my life to sit down to Christmas dinner with three Israelis, two Germans and a Muslim, least of all in a walled city at the back end of China with screaming seventies' heavy metal clobbering my eardrums, but I did that night. At the other end of the room, some young Japanese men were intently drinking themselves senseless. Halfway through the night, one of them tried to stand up and crashed headlong across the table. The first half of the day was beginning to look almost normal.

The next morning, in the company of David, a student from Brisbane misguided enough to want to come with me, I kept heading west.

'The "Eagle Nest Barrier" on the road between Yunnan and Tali'

The village of Yingwuguan, between Kunming and Dali

ABOVE AND TOP RIGHT: 'Memorial in the Temple of the Goddess of Mercy, near Tali-fu'

Bai woman, Dali

Dali and Erhai Lake

Top and bottom: 'Snow-clad mountains behind Tali'

Village market

Old man smoking a pipe

中国

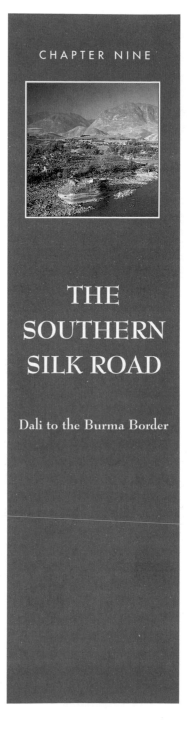

As we left the city we passed the temple to Guanyin, the Goddess of Mercy, patron goddess of travellers. One hundred years ago Morrison stopped here for tea. I said a quick prayer. I was heading for Burma, and it looked as if I was going to need her help.

CHAPTER NINE

THE SOUTHERN SILK ROAD

Dali to the Burma Border

Remains of the suspension bridge
over the Salween River

In a booth reeking of cigarette smoke at the Dali post office two days before, I had stood for upwards of an hour listening to the whirrs and pops on the line as I tried to call the Ministry of Hotels and Tourism, Union of Myanmar. I had just about nodded off to sleep when the distinctive fuzz of a long-distance connection told me that I was about to get through. It was answered by U Myo Lwin himself, Deputy Director General of Hotels and Tourism. (*U* means 'mister' in Burmese, more or less).

'It's Angus McDonald here. Do you remember that I applied some time ago to cross from China into Myanmar at Bhamo? I am a writer,' I shouted into the mouthpiece.

'Yes, I remember. Actually, this matter has not been decided. You will have to wait.'

'But it's been four months! When do you think ...?' And then the line died. I tried again for another half hour before giving up in frustration.

Four months before, I had started my journey in Rangoon, where I had gone specifically to check out the possibility of this border crossing. The junta that runs Burma is not noted for its fondness for writers, any more than for the efficiency of its bureaucracy, let alone the peaceful, enlightened administration of its remoter borders. This, I had known from the outset, was going to be the trickiest part of the whole project.

But I also knew that although the generals of the SLORC — the State Law and Order Restoration Council, Burma's government — might control the country with an iron fist and not even the pretence of a velvet glove, they were susceptible to at least one thing I had it in my power to offer them: Johnnie Walker Black Label.

Unfortunately, in the event I only had Red Label, courtesy of Bangkok Airport duty free. Maybe that was the problem.

Through contacts in the capital, I had managed to line up an interview with Myo Lwin. Outside, the sky was heavy with the clouds of monsoon, and the season had turned his office into a dank, dark box which looked as though it hadn't had a lick of paint since the British left in 1948. The Deputy Director was an army man but he greeted me in a white shirt and a *longyi*, the sarong that nearly all Burmese wear. I laid the bottle not very subtly on his coffee table and explained my plans to him. I told him about this book. I didn't tell him that I was writing for a newspaper.

'This will be difficult,' he said, 'but it may be possible. This border was closed for a long time. As you know, in Myanmar there are what we call white areas, which the government controls, and black areas, where we are fighting the rebels. This is a black area — there has been a lot of fighting there. But for some time now it has been peaceful. Many Chinese and Burmese are now crossing this border. So far, no foreigner has crossed it, but we are planning to allow it in the future, if the situation continues to improve. Last year we permitted an Austrian man to visit Bhamo — his name was Mr Klein, and he was writing a guidebook. As you are a writer, perhaps your book will help to promote tourism to Myanmar, yes?'

'Yes.'

'Then perhaps the Minister will give you permission. I suggest you make a formal application and give it to me.'

I went back to my hosts' house, typed up an application in quadruplicate, and dropped it back at the Ministry that afternoon. By the time I'd travelled the breadth of China, I figured, they would surely have an answer. But now, as I neared the area, the reality of the situation finally began to take hold: it didn't make much difference what the Burmese government said or did, because it simply didn't control most of the border. Apart from one narrow strip where the Burma Road connects the two countries, the area was held by warlords and rebel armies. The particular spot that I was aiming for was controlled by a group called the Kachin Independence Army — or at least to the best of my knowledge it was. Researching the question in Australia and Bangkok, I hadn't even been able to get a decent map of the place.

But for the time being the Kachin Independence Army was the least of my difficulties. Right now our bus was staring up the back of a truck, and the truck was going nowhere.

David and I got out to have a look. Soon after leaving Xia Guan, the city guarding the southern entrance to the Dali valley, the country had changed abruptly once again. We had entered a steep gorge where a river flowed fast and white below us, and I counted three hydro-electric dams in quick succession. The country was rough, the road narrow; we'd been going for about an hour when we ground to a halt. We were at the back of a long queue that consisted of trucks, cars, trucks, jeeps, trucks, buses, trucks, trucks and trucks. At the top, two trucks had caught each other as they rounded a blind corner. Nothing serious, but the road was blocked. The drivers had both disappeared.

After half an hour or so our bus made a tortuous U-turn on the narrow road, inching backwards and forwards between the cutting on one side and the drop to the river on the other, and headed back for Xia Guan. We got our packs out and hiked up to the head of the queue. The afternoon was warm and peaceful, and we kept walking. After a kilometre or two we came across a little camp of road workers. I'd carried my load about as far as I was able, and we sat down for a rest and a bowl of hot water. A woman was cooking lunch in a makeshift kitchen, tipping bucketfuls of pork and vegetables into a giant wok and stirring it with a small shovel. Every once in a while she'd turn around and beam at us as David and I swapped travel tales, his from Africa and mine from India.

The cook, smiling, handed us two bowls of steaming rice and vegetables, and refused our offers of payment. Then it was time to think about moving on. Unfortunately, neither of us had the vaguest clue where we were, let alone how we were going to get out of there. We were just starting to ponder this when a four-wheel-drive jeep rounded the bend. The accident must have been cleared. We put out our thumbs and, to our surprise, it stopped to pick us up.

We felt like visiting VIPs in a black limousine as the jeep gobbled up the miles. Sometimes we'd have to stop as teams of labourers quarried stone from cliffs beside the road, blocking the highway with their trailers. Streaming in either direction up and down the narrow road was a never-ending procession of Dongfengs, the uniform squarish trucks, always painted a monotone blue or green or beige, that teem across the face of China by the million. *Dongfeng* means 'East Wind', which strikes me as a poetic name for a very prosaic vehicle.

The mountains got steeper, thinly covered with stunted pine trees or just coarse khaki grass, and the rivers faster, and the country ever more lonely and beautiful as evening approached and we dozed off in the back of the jeep. Then we topped a pass and the road became wider and smoother and we drove through a patch of forest which ended where a large village sat on the shores of a long narrow turquoise lake, and suddenly we were in a rich open plain ringed by mountains. We thundered down the broad straight highway like a jet about to take off, heading towards a cluster of concrete just visible up at the other end of the valley, and then we were in Baoshan, our destination. We paid the driver, said thanks and went looking for a bed.

That night, I sat writing and David watched television. The TV was showing a special about Mao; it was the old boy's hundredth birthday at last. A century's worth of grainy black and white documentary footage, war, famine, the Long March, planes, caps with stars on them, soldiers in puttees, parades, dams, power stations, cheering crowds, ballistic missiles, Richard Nixon and Deng Xiaoping flitted across the screen, leaving me no wiser than before. I got out my maps again.

From Dali to the Burmese border runs a series of parallel north–south ridges up to 3,500 metres (11,482 feet) high, intercut by deep valleys in which flow the Mekong, the Salween and the Shweli Rivers, rushing down from their mountain sources on their way to water the plains and paddy fields of South-East Asia. The highway runs east–west, cutting directly across the grain of the land like a massive rollercoaster; even Morrison found this stretch tough going, a hard, remote no-man's land peopled by hardy tribespeople and the occasional lonely Chinese garrison.

The first river Morrison had to cross was the Mekong, known in China as the Lancang Jiang. According to his account, the crossing was at a fine old suspension bridge over a deep gorge between the villages of Shuizhai and Shanyang. I looked for them on the map. Following the line of the river with my finger, they turned out to be two little dots, well south of the modern highway. According to my guidebook, the bridge was built in 1475, on a route that was pioneered in the second century BC as China's first great imperial dynasty, the Han, struck out to the south-west looking for a trade route to India. It also said that the bridge was still intact. How we were going to get to it, I had no idea.

I awoke to the busy bustle of dawn and the clanging of yet more roadworks and yet more construction sites. The Chinese established their first garrison here in AD 69, I thought incoherently as I struggled out of bed and gave David a shake; surely they can't still be building?!

We visited the bus station first and, having drawn a blank there, began to ask the driver of every vehicle we came across if they could take us to Shuizhai. To make sure there was no mistake, I pointed at the name of the village on my map. Finally, a man in a little white minibus agreed to take us. After ten minutes, we pulled off on to a secondary road. The driver asked to look at the map again. Then he asked directions from some locals. Then he asked me again exactly where we wanted to go. I told him I wanted to see the Jihong Qiao — the Rainbow Bridge. He told me that it had disappeared, destroyed by a flood some time in the 1980s. This was a blow, but I still wanted to get there.

My Chinese was fast nearing the limits of its usefulness as he pointed to various points on the map and gestured that the road was blocked. Could we get to Shanyang, then — the village on the far side of the river? He seemed to think we could. David, who spoke no Chinese at all and had only been in the country a week, sat there looking as if he was wondering what he'd got himself into. We turned round and rejoined the highway. Heading back in the direction we had come from the night before, we drove past the lake and through the forest, the road deteriorating painfully as we went. At the bottom of the pass we came to the point where the Mekong twists out of the mountains to join the highway briefly before plunging south again. At a roadside restaurant, the driver made some more enquiries.

He asked everyone from the cook to a pair of policemen on a massive motorbike with a sidecar and a red light sticking up on top of a little pole. When he came back he told us that from here the only way to Shanyang was by a path that followed the opposite bank of the river. From where we sat we could see the path, a scar through the forest on a steep hillside. Could we drive up there? No, he told us, it was far too rough to drive. He wanted to go back to Baoshan. We would have to walk. How far is it? I asked. About 30 kilometres (19 miles), he thought. Or maybe 40 (25 miles).

We ate a solid lunch at the restaurant and resigned ourselves to a long hike and a night out in the middle of nowhere, while our friend smoked four cigarettes in quick succession through a massive bamboo water pipe. Then he took us down to a bridge that crossed the river near by and dropped us off.

We walked across the bridge. The path turned out to be a graded road wide enough for a semitrailer. A group of peasants were sitting nearby, and I went and asked one of them how we could get to Shanyang. There was a bus, he told me. It came twice a day from Baoshan. The next one wouldn't be till the evening. And how far was it? Twenty kilometres (12 miles), I was told. We started to walk.

After an hour a boy of about fifteen putt-putted along at the helm of a walking tractor, one of those outboard trailers, seen everywhere in China, that are basically a motorised version of the pony cart. We flagged him down and asked if he was going as far as Shanyang. Yes, he told us with a broad grin; we jumped on the back. For another hour the dust and exhaust fumes flew in our faces as we bounced around on the suspensionless steel tray and our chauffeur gave it as much throttle as the little machine could muster. By the time we finally pulled into Shanyang my kidneys felt as if they'd been through a blender and everything from the soles of my boots to the top of my head was filthy with dust. David was the same.

It was four o'clock. By my estimation, it was somewhere between 5 and 10 kilometres (3 and 6 miles) to the river. If we wanted to find the bridge and be back at the village before nightfall, we didn't have a minute to waste. I asked at the village shop where to find the Jihong Qiao, and was pointed to a footpath. We strode down it like a couple of Olympic walkers, quickly leaving the village behind and striking out across the fields. We ascended one slope and ran stumbling down the other side, into a valley that was like a terracotta bowl with a glaze of green paddy at the bottom. Skirting the base of the depression, we passed through another small village and began to climb again. Farmers were bringing cattle back down from the day's grazing, raising small clouds of red dust that caught in our already parched throats. The path was a deep gash carved into the hillside by centuries of use, and I realised that we were probably on the old highway.

As we neared the top of the rise, worn flagstones began to appear, and for a minute or two we were walking along a five-foot-wide paved footpath that led from nowhere to nowhere in the middle of nowhere. Then, at the top of the pass, there was a crumbling arch and the remains of a wall. Three blue–grey tiles, each carved with an elegant ideograph in the old style, were set into the brickwork above the arch, which wore its years as easily as it wore the golden rays of the five o'clock sun. My best guess was that it was a marker for the boundary between the prefectures of Baoshan and Dali. In front of us yawned the dark chasm of the Mekong, which always has been and always will be the border between these districts, whatever they might be called in years to come.

A farmer ambled past with some sheep, glancing curiously at us as he went. But for the tiles with their fine characters, it could have been some eighteenth-century European artist's romantic impression of a classical idyll.

We took photos of each other in front of the arch, and pressed on. When we turned the next bend, the flagstones disappeared again. In the calm of evening the air was crowded with the ghosts of travellers who'd walked this path from the dawn of the Chinese empire until the Burma Road took over just fifty years ago. Generals and foot soldiers, cooks and coolies, slaves, scholars, bandits, traders and priests, all had passed this way; British colonels with waxed moustaches; Yongli, the last of the Ming, fleeing to Burma in front of the advancing Qing in 1659, only to be brought back captive two years later and put to death; Buddhist monks on their way to India in search of wisdom; mule trains heavy with silk, satin, porcelain, tobacco, tea, gold, iron and silver from Sichuan and Yunnan, or salt, cotton, amber, rubies, jade, ivory, pearls, cowry shells and peacock feathers from Burma, India and beyond; rhinos and white elephants for tribute to the emperor; Zhuge Liang, master strategist, last encountered by the deathbed of Liu Bei back in the Yangtze Gorges; Edgar Snow and C.P. Fitzgerald and Reginald Johnston, some-time tutor to the last emperor, Puyi; spies, fugitives and footloose vagabonds like me; Marco Polo himself even, on his way to Baoshan to watch Kublai Khan's battle-hardened archers decimate a force of 2,000 Burmese war elephants in an afternoon.

And where do a couple of Australians fit in to all of this? Suddenly I felt I was hard on Morrison's heels, another stranger in a strange land, the 100 years that separated us no more than a blink in this massive sweep of history.

Travellers like Morrison and I are often called on to explain ourselves. What drives us? The only thing I can ever think of to say is that I can't imagine not doing it. The only reason I'm sitting here right now writing this book, in between long periods of staring out the window at the red roofs of Bondi, is that, hopefully, it will help me to get away again soon.

But perhaps there's something else to it. Australians are some of the world's greatest wanderers. Even 100 years ago, Morrison met at least three others on his way across China. Maybe it's because white Australians, with only 200 years in a country that's about as far, psychologically and geographically, as you can get from Europe, still don't feel quite at home in Australia. Look at the way we squander scarce water trying to make our gardens look like English lawns as they frizzle in the December sun. We're constantly looking over the horizon for that lost ideal, perpetually seeking out the familiar in the strange.

Or maybe it's just that we can. Morrison was born in Victoria in 1862, at the height of the gold rush that transformed Australia from a collection of miserable convict settlements to an affluent young nation. I was born in 1962, bang in the middle of the longest period of sustained prosperity in our history, during the postwar boom when ... but now I'm just theorising. Of the thousands who must have passed this way over the centuries only two, as far as I know, had been Australian (Morrison and C.P.Fitzgerald). Now it was four.

We walked a little further, but it was obvious we'd never make it to the bottom of the gorge before nightfall. We turned around and hurried back to the village, stumbling the last couple of kilometres in the darkness. That night we slept in a grubby little room at the bottom of someone's house and ate at the only restaurant in the village, a meal of gritty rice and greasy cabbage. Older still than Chinese civilisation is the life of the Chinese peasant.

Next morning David sensibly decided to return to Baoshan. I walked back to the river.

The Chinese invented the suspension bridge, and built the first iron chain bridge at least 1,000 years before the earliest examples to appear in Europe. The design may very well have originated here in western Yunnan, where the mountains are steep and the rivers fast. The same provincial chronicle that records Zhuge Liang's visit mentions that he ordered the sinking of holes for the attachment of chains or cables at this very spot around AD 225, making it the site of one of the earliest suspension bridges on record.

At the bottom of the dark gorge where the green–brown water of the Mekong rushes silently by on its way towards Burma, Thailand, Laos, Cambodia, Vietnam and the South China Sea, I saw that the fifteenth-century Jihong Qiao, 60 metres (197 feet) long and supported by seventeen chains made of links the size of your forearm, was indeed a ruin. All that remained were the stout stone abutments protruding into the stream, the iron chains spilling down the shattered masonry where they had snapped like old rubber bands.

An old man with a leaky boat was there to paddle the occasional villager who wanted to make the crossing, bailing out the ferry each time he got to the opposite bank. I handed him a note and we went over, the flimsy vessel quivering in the stiff current. On the other side were the remains of an entry arch to the bridge and, behind it, yellow cliffs covered with the inscriptions of travellers past. I followed the path a little way up the bank, searching for the spot where Jensen had photographed the scene. It didn't take long. Looking back to the west side of the gorge, I saw that the treacherous zig-zag footpath leading from the pass down to the bridge, which I had just descended, hadn't shifted in a century. God knows how many coolies must have lost their footing on it over the centuries, ending their lives in that haunted place.

Now I had to face the prospect of climbing back up this mad slope in the full blaze of the afternoon sun. It wasn't hard to figure out why the motor road didn't come this way. By next morning I was back among the exhaust and charging trucks of the modern highway, thumbing a lift to Baoshan.

* * *

I met David back at the hotel. He had plans to go off in a different direction, so we shook hands and said we'd look out for each other back in Dali. Then I got on the bus to my next destination. I hadn't even managed to have a shower.

The bus crawled over the next hump of mountains and tumbled down the other side, through an idyllic little town called Pupiao in a valley carpeted with straw-coloured hedgerows of sugarcane, and then over another ridge, and down another set of switchbacks, and we had arrived at the village of Daojie in the Salween valley where, Chinese tradition has it, the air is foul, malarial and fatal. I had another bridge to find.

This one was a bit easier than the last. It was obvious from my maps that the highway here took much the same route as the old road. I followed the cobbled highway for twenty minutes or so till I got to the river, where a new concrete suspension bridge was guarded by an army post. Adolescents in jungle greens were checking the papers of everyone coming along the road, the innocence of their faces betrayed by the black, well-oiled steel of the automatic weapons at their sides. A sign in Chinese and English warned people not to take photos. I thought of some of the things I'd seen in the last few days: the roadworks, the new petrol stations, the building sites at Baoshan, the endless trucks. This might still be the raw backblocks of China, but someone somewhere obviously had serious plans for it.

A girl in uniform took my passport, wrote down the details, gave me a long hard look, and waved me on. I followed the river north, looking for the landforms in Jensen's photo. Half an hour later, as the sun died among the hump-backed mountains behind me, I was pretty sure I'd found them. Next morning I went and photographed what remained of the bridge: four stone abutments, minus the suspended walkway. Behind it, winding their way up the steep ridge, were more remnants of the flagged path. In front of me, the river was wide and serene and clear, mirroring the rugged mountains, just as it had done in Jensen's photo.

A couple of months after Morrison passed this way, the first shots were fired in the Sino-Japanese War, back on the east coast. By April 1895 Japan, which a few decades before had been an obscure feudal kingdom at the periphery of Asia, had smashed and humiliated its giant neighbour and ancient antagonist, taking Taiwan for booty. Japan's meteoric rise to world power status had begun.

Just fifty years later that rise would reach its high water mark here, by the banks of the Salween. With most of South-East Asia in their grasp, the Japanese began working their way up from Burma, through the back door into China. In 1942 they finally reached the end of their bit of elastic when the Chinese blew up the brand-new bridge on the Burma Road and halted their advance on Kunming, just 30 kilometres (19 miles) south of where I stood now.

Or had they? Fifty years on, I come along with ... a sackful of Japanese cameras and a Casio watch.

Morrison would later play a role in this twentieth-century drama when in 1904 he did his best to provoke the Russo-Japanese War in the hope that it would effectively end Russia's hopes to rival British influence in the Far East. Well, it did that alright. But it also foreshadowed a time when the Japanese would deal the British, Dutch and French Empires in Asia a blow from which they would never recover. I wonder if Morrison would have been so keen on the idea if he'd known that. Probably not.

I wonder too, if, in a moment of clairvoyance he had been able to see teenaged soldiers doing battle by this river, thousands of miles from home, screaming for their mothers as their blood spilled across the ruddy soil, he would have changed his course. Maybe, but probably not.

I walked back into town for breakfast. A busy market was all but blocking the highway, trucks and jeeps honking their horns hotly as they inched their way through the crowd. Pork, lettuces, incense, cloth, paper charms, green bananas and sacks of golden tobacco were changing hands. Many women were in narrow sarongs and sandals and little caps of orange or red that looked like day-glo bishops' mitres. Some of the older ones wore dark jackets and long skirts and something like a black bellhop's cap, only taller and with a scarf tied over the top.

They were Tai people, also known as the Shan, who have been radiating out of southern China for 1,000 years or more. They can be found in India, Burma, Vietnam, Laos and, of course, Thailand. The migration, it seems fair to surmise, has been motivated at least partly by the southward expansion of the Han.

'None but Shans live in the valley,' wrote Morrison, and this is confirmed by other Western travellers of the time. Not any more. In the market that day, I saw plenty of Han faces, mostly behind the stalls. The hotel I stayed in and the restaurant where I ate were also run by Han Chinese. As I devoured my noodles-and-eggs, I thought again about the highway, the soldiers, the new buildings. And about how Wudi, the great Han emperor, had ordered his troops through here in the second century BC in an early attempt to pacify the unruly local tribes and secure the trade route into Burma. There had been the occasional interruption from the British, the Japanese and one or two other upstarts over the last twenty centuries. But now, I could see, things were well and truly back to normal.

I packed up my bag, walked a kilometre or two down the road, and sat down under a tree to wait for a lift. Before long a truck pulled up, a tanker with a load of diesel. The driver, like bus and truck drivers the length of China, was wearing enormous sunglasses, a black leather jacket and grubby white cotton gloves. The familiar jam-jar of tea was at his side. I now carried a packet of high-quality Yunnan cigarettes to offer to people on such occasions, and I gave him a couple.

We crossed the bridge and began to climb almost immediately. This was the steepest ridge of them all, and the truck laboured for hours in the dust and afternoon sun, the driver flashing me grins the whole time as he fought the wheel and pumped the pedals. Trucks were pouring down the mountain towards us, nine out of ten loaded with logs, fresh and raw, some of which were so large that only two or three could fit on the tray. To ward off boredom, I started to count them. Twenty-three went by in an hour.

When we got to the top the driver switched off the engine and we descended 1,000 metres (3,280 feet) worth of loose surface hairpins on the brakes, my knuckles white against the dashboard as we sailed within inches of the timber trucks. Then we emerged once again from the forest and came to the next river, the Shweli. I stopped to get a picture of the town that looked as if it hadn't grown much since Jensen, predictably, had got a shot of its suspension bridge which, also predictably, was now a ruin. Next morning I thumbed a lift over the last of the humps to Tengchong — Tengyueh in Morrison's day — the final garrison before the Burmese border.

When I arrived I was still carrying the filth of the tractor ride to the Mekong, plus another ten layers or so on top of that. My skin was sticky like honey with congealed sweat and my jeans were so alive I was afraid they would walk to Burma by themselves if I let them out of my sight. Unfortunately, it was mid-afternoon and the hot water in the hotel didn't come on until evening, so I foisted my foulness on the main street of Tengchong as I looked for the city wall, the temple, the theatre and the old telegraph office. All gone. At seven I got back to the hotel and stood for half an hour under a spring-fed hot shower. It was even better than Jack's chocolate cake.

Glowing like a nuclear mishap and feeling almost human again, I went out to look for some food. In a place called the Mandalay Café, a group of young men dressed in padded nylon jackets, longyis, sandals and baseball caps were playing a game with cards featuring scantily-clad Western women. As I looked inside, the men noticed me and began a chorus of 'Hey! Hey, you!' I was ready to be affronted until I remembered that this is the way Burmese often greet white people in the street. I went and joined them.

None of them could speak English, but they ordered me a cup of tea and, for my listening pleasure, put a tape of Abba on the ghetto blaster. On one wall was a picture of Mao and Zhou. Facing it was a poster of Guns'n'Roses. After a while a couple more Burmese arrived. One of them introduced himself and told me, in good English, that he came up to Tengchong each year to trade. He was a schoolteacher, he said, and schoolteachers in Burma don't make enough to feed their families unless they do something on the side. His English name was John.

'Do you want to buy some jade, my friend?' he asked.

Well, I didn't really, but he pulled out some samples anyway. Each rock was the size of a fist, dark green, uncut, the veins glowing dully in the dim light. Even with my non-existent knowledge of such things, they looked beautiful.

'How much?'

'For you, $8,000.'

I took a gulp of tea. Considering a schoolteacher in Burma makes about $10 a month, this sounded like a bit more than a sideline. I knew I was expected to bargain, but even so ...

'Sell it to a Chinese,' I suggested. 'They've got plenty of money, and they like jade.'

'I know,' he said. 'I will.'

A Chinese woman had sat down behind him, and another Burmese man, and another Chinese woman. My friend began speaking in Chinese that was as fluent as his English.

'This is my wife. Actually I have two wives, one in Burma, one in China.' He grinned.

'Do many Burmese come to China?' I asked.

'Oh yes,' he said. 'We come to trade. The main items of trade are jade, heroin and wood.' I remembered the trucks loaded with timber. The drugs were, presumably, a little less conspicuous. 'These things come from the mountains on the border. The government has no control there, only the local armies. Some people are getting very rich.'

A slight shudder went through me as it hit home where I was heading. I was going to have to watch my step from now on, I realised, if I didn't want to end up impaled on one of the sharper ends of the Golden Triangle.

Someone else had started to pester me. He had on a camouflage cap and his eyes had a glassy, vaguely maniacal stare that I didn't like. He was so drunk he could barely speak.

'This man is a fighter,' said John. 'He was a corporal in the CPB — the Communist Party of Burma.' The CPB, I recalled, had controlled a large enclave just over the border from the late 1960s until it collapsed in 1989 from a combination of ethnic rivalries, jungle fatigue and sheer geriatric irrelevance.

A little later John and his friends disappeared into the night, to do what dodgy deals I do not know. This left me with the corporal, whose social skills by this time amounted to long periods staring past my ear interspersed with the occasional slurred suggestion like 'drink' and 'bar' and 'girl' and 'karaooeee ...' It was New Year's Eve, and the best offer I had for a night out was to go and sing karaoke somewhere with this near-paralytic relic of a defunct insurgency. I paid for my dinner and went to bed.

* * *

There was one more of Jensen's photos yet to find. It was of the southern end of Tengchong and the surrounding hills, taken from the now disappeared city wall. I identified the line of the hill easily enough on my first afternoon, and the next morning found the place where the picture must have been taken. There was a three-storey apartment block standing on the spot. I climbed the stairs, surprising numerous families at their breakfast, found a vantage point on a top floor balcony, and ticked it off the list.

'Tengyueh is so situated that the invading army coming from Burma will find a pleasant pastime in shelling it from the open hills all around the town,' wrote Morrison. No prizes for guessing which invading army he might have been thinking of; Upper Burma had been in the hands of the British since 1885. Showing that grasp of diplomatic niceties that would serve him so well in years to come, he wrote that, 'the delimitation of the frontier of Burma is not yet complete. No time could be more opportune for its completion than the present, when China is distracted by her difficulties with Japan. China disheartened could need but little persuasion to accede to the just demand of England that the frontier of Burma shall be the true south-western frontier of China — the Salween River.' I've no idea where he picked up this last notion.

* * *

If you had the right kind of boat and permission from two governments and an insurgent army, you could paddle all the way from Tengchong to Rangoon — and on into the Bay of Bengal and beyond for that matter. From Tengchong the Daying River flows across the border to join the Irrawaddy River at Bhamo, which in turn becomes the major artery of Burma, navigable the year round. It wasn't hard to see why 2,500 years' worth of trade had funnelled out of south-west China through here on its way to Burma, India and beyond. Or why the Brits had been keen to build a railway through here in Morrison's day; or why they'd decided to annex Upper Burma, for that matter. The nearest Treaty port was 1,500 kilometres (930 miles) in the other direction over roads we've already heard enough about. And the French were busy ensconcing themselves in Vietnam, which placed them in an advantageous position to dominate the trade of Yunnan.

Unfortunately, I had neither a boat nor the requisite paperwork to get me over the border and, from the look of my map, the trail was beginning to peter out. The only highway across the border was the Burma Road, which had forked off to the south after Baoshan. Following Morrison's route, there was a road as far as the town of Yingjiang; from Yingjiang to Manyun there was a thin brown line on my map that signified 'Secondary road, cart track, path'; and from Manyun to the border, about 30 kilometres (19 miles) beyond, there was nothing at all. At least it was downhill all the way.

After a cold, foggy, early morning ride of about four hours, I got out at Yingjiang (then known as Santa) where Morrison had taken tea with a Shan prince. A cluster of minibuses was standing at a corner and I asked if they were going to Manyun. They said yes and I jumped on board to join a bunch of cheerful Shan women, their teeth stained and corroded with betel juice, and some chickens. We bounced along a dusty road through a plain of yellow grass, with banyan trees and buffalo and bamboo houses with pitched roofs. Border or no border, I suddenly knew I was back in South-East Asia.

I had lunch in Manyun, where there was a market dense with Shans and one or two Lesu, another minority, looking like birds of paradise in their richly coloured outfits, and thumbed a lift onwards. The road was suddenly rough and deserted. After an hour, we pulled over at a tiny Han village; this was as far as my driver was going. Up ahead, the rutted track wound away through forested ridges.

As I emerged from the van I was grabbed almost bodily and made to sit down in the middle of a big gathering. Women came from a kitchen with steaming ladles full of food and men and children surrounded me, whispering and smoking and smiling. Some kind of festivity was going on; people were wearing long white cotton robes and elaborate headdresses folded from the same material. I ate enough to be polite and then went to find out what was happening. Incense was being burned in front of a heavy wooden box painted red and blue; men were kneeling and an old woman was wailing. It was a funeral which, in ancestor-worshipping China, can be a spectacular event. I watched the proceedings all afternoon, while people offered me cigarettes and posed for photos. I got the impression there hadn't been a foreigner through here for quite some time.

* * *

A Han funeral, near the Burma border

As I sat writing in the village restaurant that evening, watched by what appeared to be every teenager in the district, I pondered the situation. I estimated I was between 10 and 20 kilometres (6 and 12 miles) from the border. All I had to do was keep heading west until I found out just who *did* control the bit of Burma that lay over the frontier. This was either going to be the Kachin Independence Army, AK-47 wielding hill people who hadn't seen many white faces since they took to the jungle to fight for an independent state in 1961, or the government they were up against, the SLORC, one of the most brutal, repressive regimes in the world.

> We had left the valley of the peaceful Shans and were in the forest inhabited by other 'protected barbarians' of China — the wild tribes of Kachins, who even in Burma are slow to recognise the beneficent influences of British frontier administration.

I couldn't predict how either party would react to a lone Westerner blundering unannounced into their territory, possibly while they were in the middle of delicate peace negotiations. But I could make an educated guess. Anyone who's expecting an exciting, death-defying climax at this crucial point, three-quarters of the way through the book, is going to be disappointed. Next morning, after a night spent nearly freezing under an inadequate quilt in a bamboo hut, I did exactly what any sane person would have done under the circumstances: I hitched back to Tengchong.

The day after, I was up at five to catch a bus. Somewhere around lunchtime, between Tengchong and Baoshan, a child threw up in my lap. Somewhere around afternoon tea, between Baoshan and Yongping, we got a flat tyre on an inside wheel. When I finally stumbled into Dali long after dark that night, it was like crawling back into the womb.

'The descent to the river Mekong'

'A wonderful pathway zigzags down the face of the mountain to the river, in an almost vertical incline of 2,000 ft.'

Remains of the fifteenth-century Jihong chain bridge across the Mekong

Inscriptions by past travellers on cliffs behind the Jihong bridge

The author on the old highway, above the Mekong gorge

'The River Salween, the former boundary between China and Burma'

Remains of a suspension bridge over the Salween

中国

'The suburb beyond the south side of Tengyueh'

Tengchong

'Opium smoking'

Chasing the dragon: heroin use in Dali

It seems as though I spent the next

two days back at the post office,

a greasy phone clamped to my ear,

waiting to talk to Burma.

Finally, the receiver sang with

static and I heard a faint 'Hello?'

It was Myo Lwin.

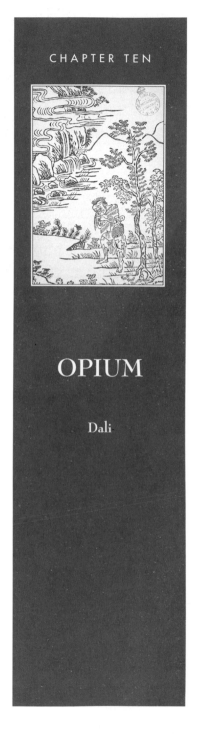

CHAPTER TEN

OPIUM

Dali·

'The opium smoker of romance'

'U Myo Lwin? This is Angus McDonald. Has my application to enter Myanmar at Bhamo been approved?'

'This has still not yet been decided. This matter has to go to the Minister.'

'Can you take it to the Minister, please?'

'The Minister is out of town presently. I suggest that you try again after about one week.'

And the line died again. We had been speaking for one minute and twenty seconds. The strange land of Myanmar was receding over the horizon.

Outside, a fierce wind was blowing down from the mountain, propelling a cloud of dust straight across town from an ancient stone house that was being demolished. I ducked into a café and spent the afternoon playing backgammon with an eccentric Englishman named Paul, who had lugged his board and custom-made dice and a big heavy book about strategy all the way from Hong Kong. I didn't win a game. Sitting with my back to the warm sun and drinking fresh-brewed Yunnan coffee, I can't say it bothered me.

Night fell eventually, and it was time to move on to Jack's, where I ran into David, also back from the wilds, and ordered a bottle of Dali beer. Maybe a week cooling my heels here wouldn't be so bad after all.

I had now traced Morrison's entire journey across China, practically every step of the way. But there was one thing I still hadn't found.

> During the nine months that I was in China I saw thousands of opium-smokers, but I never saw one to whom could be applied that description by Lay (of the British and Foreign Bible Society), so often quoted, of the typical opium-smoker in China 'with his lank and shrivelled limbs, tottering gait, sallow visage, feeble voice, and death-boding glance of eye, proclaiming him the most forlorn creature that treads upon the ground'.
>
> This fantastic description, paraded for years past for our sympathy, can be only applied to an infinitesimal number of the millions in China who smoke opium. It is a well-known fact that should a Chinese suffering from the extreme emaciation of disease be also in the habit of using the opium-pipe, it is the pipe and not the disease that in ninety-nine cases out of a hundred will be wrongly blamed as the cause of the emaciation.

Morrison here has at least two well-measured targets in his sights: one, the missionary organisations, who at the time were campaigning vigorously to end the export of Indian opium to China; and two, anybody else who got in the way of the British Empire.

中国

China in 1894 was in fact as saturated with the drug as a poem by Baudelaire or a track by Velvet Underground. It was smoked by everyone from rag-and-bone labourers to plump mandarins in soft silk. Estimates differed widely, but even those who profited by the trade had to admit that at least ten per cent of adult males were addicted to opium, their health suffering severely as a result. A good many more smoked in moderation. In Chongqing alone, the city where Morrison was moved to make his confident assertion, there were 1,230 opium shops. This is all according to the British government's *Royal Commission on Opium* which, when Morrison began his journey, was sweating its way across northern India, gathering material to decide if the trade should be banned, as some groups were urging.

Although it was the British who had first made opium affordable to all classes, there is no doubt that China by this time supplied the bulk of its own opium, cultivating it in a vast golden crescent stretching from Guizhou through Yunnan, Sichuan, Gansu, Shaanxi and Shanxi. Superior Indian opium was only for the rich; the rest smoked the local stuff, of which the best came from the cool, subtropical mountains of Yunnan. Again, estimates are unreliable, but one academic has calculated that in 1906 about seventeen per cent of arable land in Yunnan was under the poppy.

Edgar Snow, passing through around 1930, wrote:

> The Yunnanese had a saying that, 'The Chinese own the plains, the tribesmen own the mountains, the bandits own the road.' But it was the poppy that really ruled Yunnan. On the plains between Yunnanfu and Tali about half the acreage was planted for opium. For years afterward opium taxes of various kinds provided the chief source of revenue. Local magistrates usually fixed the amount of land to be devoted to poppies, the ratio depending on how much they had paid for their appointments. Often peasant tillers could *avoid* planting poppies only by paying a 'fine' — to the Opium Suppression Bureau.

The drug was used for everything from socialising, to suicide, to sealing a business deal; it killed the boredom of the mandarin and the agony of the coolie, and it was far and away the most lucrative cash crop. Light enough to be carried in quantity over the mountain trails and in demand everywhere, opium was a currency in itself, a cornerstone of the economy of western China.

Judging by the recommendations of the Commission, Morrison was far from alone when he argued that the restriction of exports from India would do little to solve China's opium problem. He also wasn't the only qualified medical man of his time to claim that opium was harmless if taken in moderation. He may well have been the only one, though, to have driven an opium-eating coolie whom he acknowledged to be dying from the addiction, at forced pace and with a 60-pound (27-kilogram) load, over that punishing sawblade of a road from Dali to Bhamo for a carefully recorded payment of 12 shillings. The fact that the coolie, whom Morrison nicknamed 'Bones', was killing himself with Chinese, not Indian, opium, apparently made it OK.

Opium was suppressed briefly after 1906, only to re-emerge as widely as ever between the wars. During its brief period of independence in the 1920s and 1930s, Yunnan was able to stabilise its currency with silver bought from the proceeds of opium sales to the rest of China. Then, after 1949, in one of the communists' more remarkable achievements, it seems to have just disappeared. In the space of a couple of years, tens of millions of addicts were rehabilitated — or else died, presumably — and the poppy was eradicated from the face of China. It didn't move far away, though.

* * *

Down a narrow back lane on the far side of Dali from the Protestant church where I had spent Christmas, is the Catholic church, which dates from the 1920s. When I found it after half an hour fossicking down tortuous alleys, it turned out to be a structural hybrid, an architectural equivalent of the dogged French or Portuguese missionary in his flowing robes and queue. From the outside it looked like a cross between a Hollywood haunted house and a minor pavilion in the Forbidden City, the faded timber of its belfry thrusting up from a winged roof decorated with what looked like dragon's tails and supported by a framework of intricately interlocked and painted wood panels. The entrance was between two red pillars carved with ideographs, behind which lay an arched stone doorway that would have looked at home in a mediaeval cathedral. Inside was a riot of brightly coloured images of the saints and a ceiling painted to look like a starry night.

An attendant who must have been in her eighties, nearly deaf and nearly blind, gave me a brief look around, and locked the gates again. As I stood in the deserted forecourt admiring the facade, something else caught my eye. At the bottom of a wall in a corner lay a used hypodermic, with congealing blood still in its chamber.

In another part of town was an old teahouse which I got into the habit of visiting for an hour or two in the afternoons. It had rickety deckchairs and stone tables and weeds growing through the tiles in the roof, and a nice old lady in an apron and chef's hat would bring you tea in a white porcelain mug for half a yuan, the green water steaming with a subtle flavour when you lifted the lid for a sip. In the smoky front room old men gambled on games of mah-jong, while out the back there were usually some lads and sometimes a couple of heavily made-up young women, always absorbed in cards. Most of the youngsters looked in worse shape than the grandads.

On about my third visit, I sat for longer than usual and just watched. Three or four men in their twenties were lolling about silently in their deckchairs, thick coats pulled up about their ears in spite of the warm afternoon sun. Some of their friends were playing cards. The old woman did a round to replenish everyone's cup, and went inside again. Then a boy sitting in a corner pulled a piece of foil from a cigarette packet and held a lighter to it, burning the paper from underneath. This done, he took a little packet from his pocket and sprinkled something on the foil. Then he held the lighter beneath the foil as he drew the smoke in through a cardboard tube.

I pulled an instamatic from my pocket and quickly took a picture. Then I got out. It didn't look too much like the opium den pictured in Morrison's book, but it was near enough. The powder they were smoking, as I was to confirm later, was heroin.

* * *

When the communists took over in Yunnan, the remnants of the shattered Guomindang army couldn't exactly join their comrades in Taiwan, separated from them as they were by 2,000 kilometres (1,243 miles) of hostile territory and the Formosa Strait. So they went the only way they could: over the border and into the dense snarl of mountains where Burma bulges east to meet Laos, one of the most impenetrable places on earth, a country of gorges and jungles and head-hunting hilltribes which theoretically belonged to Burma but where anyone with a powerful enough army could hack out their own little kingdom.

According to Burma expert Bertil Lintner, the only Westerner to visit much of this area in recent times, this is what happened next:

> Led by General Li Mi, [the Guomindang] invaded Kengtung
> State, the eastern-most of the [Burmese] Shan States. In
> January 1950, remnants of the 93rd Division, the 26th Division
> and General Li Mi's own 8th Army arrived in the southern
> Shan States and ensconced themselves in the hilly region
> surrounding Mong Hsat near the Thai–Burmese border. They
> recruited soldiers from the border areas, mostly hill-tribesmen,
> and began collecting arms, ammunition and provisions from
> sources outside Burma.
>
> The number of KMT [Guomindang] troops in the Shan States
> swelled from about 1,700 in early 1950 to 4,000 in April 1951.
> The tiny Mong Hsat airstrip, built during World War Two, was
> reconstructed into a formidable air base capable of receiving
> C-46 and C-47 transport planes, which brought in munitions
> and medical supplies from Bangkok and Taipei. This dramatic

build-up was a joint venture between the KMT government on the island of Taiwan and the US security authorities. The aim was to reconquer the Chinese mainland from the communists, using the bases in northeastern Shan States as springboards. The Kengtung-based 'Secret KMT Army' tried on no less than seven occasions between 1950 and 1952 to invade Yunnan but was repeatedly driven back into the Shan States; it never managed to penetrate more than a few miles beyond the Sino-Burmese frontier ...

The KMT also coerced the farmers into growing opium and introduced a hefty opium tax, which forced the impoverished hill-tribe farmers to grow even more in order to make ends meet. The annual production increased from a mere 30 tons at the time of Burma's independence in 1948 to 600 tons in the mid 1950s. In its reports to the UN, the Burmese government alleged that much of the opium was air-lifted from Mong-Hsat to Taiwan by US planes. However, opium was not an international problem at that time and, apart from the then democratic authorities in Burma, few paid much attention to the CIA's assistance to the KMT's trade in narcotics. Ensuring General Li Mi's loyalty to the 'secret war' against China was a far more important consideration for the US security planners. Some years later, another KMT general, Tuan Shi-wen, explained the Nationalist Chinese involvement in the Shan opium trade: 'We have to continue to fight the evil of communism and to fight you must have an army, and an army must have guns, and to buy guns you must have money. In these mountains the only money is opium.'

The Golden Triangle, which today produces perhaps two-thirds of the world's illegal opiates, had come into existence. Which is ironic considering that the Americans were then in the habit of alleging, with no foundation whatsoever, that the Chinese communists were flooding the capitalist countries with narcotics to soften vigilance against the diabolical revolution they were hellbent on exporting.

* * *

I returned to the teashop the next day with Chris, an Australian who'd just been studying in Shanghai and who spoke good Chinese. The young men were there as usual, staring into space. I caught the eye of one of the more alert ones, who had nodded to me on previous visits. When he stepped outside with a friend, I asked if he wouldn't mind talking. I went back and got Chris, and we followed the pair of them through a maze of back streets.

We stopped behind a building, Chris interpreting as I explained that I wanted to interview them for a newspaper story, that I wouldn't take any photos or use any names, and that the story would be published in English in a foreign newspaper. With a little inducement, they agreed to cooperate.

One of them was a wreck, with flaky skin, filthy hair and bloodshot eyes. He didn't say a word the whole time. But his friend was more forthcoming. He pointed out the trackmarks on his arm and carried his little packet of smack openly in his hand as he walked about the streets. I got the impression that he took a perverse pride in his habit, that he showed it off in a gesture of romantic, nihilistic protest. Protest against what, I don't know, though I can think of a few possibilities. Perhaps that's why he agreed to talk.

We carried on, the two men walking a bit ahead of us, taking a roundabout route in a melodramatic attempt to be inconspicuous that only made me more edgy. Finally we came to a reservoir on the edge of town and sat down on the embankment. Ponies were grazing on the grass and drinking the water. In front of us was the dark bulk of Cangshan, its nineteen snow-frosted peaks like a cresting wave on a moonlit night. Behind were the lush fields where Morrison said he saw poppies as tall as himself, 'probably unequalled in the world', and beyond that, the thin cool strip of Erhai Lake.

Hu, as I will call him, immediately pulled out a needle and went down to mix his fix with murky water from the reservoir. His friend followed later. As Hu rolled up his trousers and stuck the syringe into his knee, I asked questions while Chris interpreted. The more of the stuff Hu pumped into himself, the less coherent his answers became. All the while, I looked nervously around for the policeman I was sure was about to appear over the brow of the embankment and throw us all in jail.

Dali, Hu told us, had five or six hundred users. He and his friend had been using for seven or eight years, during which time the drug had always been readily available. Both of them were unemployed.

'*Ni pa aidzi bing ma?*' asked Chris — 'Are you afraid of getting Aids?'

'*Bu pa.*' — 'I'm not afraid.' Each had his own needle.

'What happens if you're caught?' I asked Chris to ask him.

That depends, Hu replied. Rich people can just pay off the police. If you don't have money, it depends on your attitude. If you want to be reformed, they put you into compulsory rehabilitation. If not, it's the *laogai* — forced labour camp. And if they catch you with more than 50 grams (2 ounces), they assume you're a dealer and they shoot you.

I was already aware of this last detail, but its repetition didn't do anything to ease my mood.

'How old are you?'

'Twenty-seven,' he told Chris. 'My friend is thirty. I don't expect to live past thirty-five. I don't care ...'

His grip on the conversation was slipping fast. He told us other things, but I can't vouch for their reliability. Before long, I slipped them each a note and we left them to it.

* * *

As time went on and the soldiers grew older and the possibility of taking China back from the communists receded, the Guomindang remnants in that malarial no-man's land they had wrested from Burma settled down and tended their fields and watched their kids grow up. Most of them were eventually kicked out in 1968 when the Chinese-backed Communist Party of Burma invaded the area, but even the CPB found it couldn't survive without cultivating opium. To this day much of the heroin trade out of the Golden Triangle is controlled by ethnic Chinese.

In the 1980s, as China liberalised its economy and normalised relations with Burma, and particularly after the CPB splintered in 1989, the borders were thrown open to trade. Yunnan went into a kind of boom as the consumer goods that the neglected Burmese economy was incapable of producing — bicycles, televisions, toothpaste and 1,000 other things — funnelled out, and primary produce — rice, timber and gems — flooded in. With them came heroin.

Most of the heroin exported from the Golden Triangle used to leave via Thailand. But as that way became more dangerous, the long but little-policed overland route through China became more attractive. Up to half of the heroin that leaves the Golden Triangle may now exit through China via Hong Hong, Beijing and Shanghai, carrying on to Tokyo, Los Angeles, Sydney. Which could well mean that the old Burma Road now has the distinction of being the artery that bears the single greatest volume of narcotics anywhere in the world.

The Beijing government admits that there are 250,000 registered addicts in the country. This can probably safely be extrapolated to a real figure of more than a million, which is a good deal less than the ten per cent of adult males who were addicted to opium in 1894. But the output of the Golden Triangle is growing, law enforcement in China is in decline, unemployment is on the rise, and the Burma border trade is flourishing. There was also, of course, no Aids in Morrison's day.

In 1991 the government launched a nationwide crackdown on drug abuse. That year, according to Amnesty International, at least 252 death sentences were handed down for drug offences in Yunnan alone. There were a number of executions at Xia Guan, the administrative capital of Dali Prefecture.

'Edicts are still issued against the use of opium,' wrote Morrison in 1894.

* * *

On the morning of 11th January I spent another two hours at the Dali post office trying to get through to Rangoon. Finally, that afternoon, I got through to Myo Lwin from a private phone in a restaurant.

'Has the Minister approved my application?' I asked without wasting a second.

'No, this matter has still not yet been decided.'

'But I must have a decision straightaway. I cannot stay in China much longer.'

'Then I suggest you cancel your trip.'

'But I ...'

But but but ... I had been cut off, the veil had dropped again, and Burma disappeared once more into the twilight of antiquated communications and self-imposed isolation.

Next morning I packed my bag, extended my visa, rescheduled my flights, said goodbye to the friends I had made in Dali and took off again down the Burma Road, this time visiting the towns of Lojie, Ruili and Wanding, all of which are centres for the cross-border trade. In Lojie, a small village with a banyan tree in the middle that marked the border, I came across a strange place populated by Shans, Chinese and Burmese, with bars, drugs and a cinema showing pornographic films. At a long series of gambling tables, Chinese and Burmese alike crowded to play and stallholders sat with plastic trays stuffed with Burmese *kyats* (the everyday currency of Burma, pronounced *chats*) and Chinese renminbi. I walked a kilometre or two into Burmese territory until I came to a checkpost, where an immigration official greeted me by saying, 'Aha, I think you are being a correspondent!' and summoned some mates to escort me straight back out again.

Ruili was a mess of construction and makeshift karaoke bars where jade and rubies were traded by the handful in the street and young Burmese men were trying to scam the Chinese in any way they could. Wanding was a dusty and uninspiring collection of concrete, for all that it might be the greatest clearing house for heroin in the world, with a cluster of refineries just over the border. Yet, even when I could see it just across the river, Burma seemed as distant as ever.

And then I had to ride 1,000 kilometres (621 miles) back to Kunming in those pulverising buses, and then fly 1,200 kilometres (746 miles) to Bangkok, and then fly another 600 kilometres (373 miles) to Rangoon, from where, if I could by some miracle screw the permission out of the Ministry, I would make my way another 1,000 kilometres to Bhamo. In other words, to within 50 kilometres (30 miles) of where I had abandoned my trek on the Chinese side.

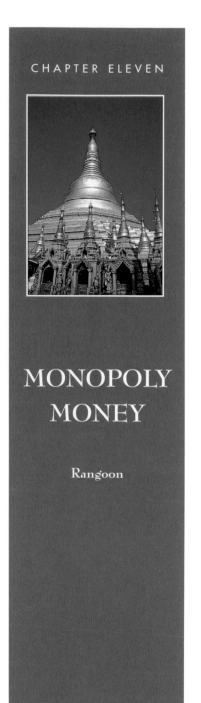

CHAPTER ELEVEN

MONOPOLY MONEY

Rangoon

It takes about an hour and a half to fly from Bangkok to Rangoon, but when you get off the plane you feel as if you've stepped back into the Asia of Somerset Maugham. The terminal buildings are low and white and weather-worn and there are funny old propeller planes parked around the place. You could almost imagine Lord Mountbatten wandering about, all uniform pants and scrambled egg cap, or bare-chested soldiers in Bombay bloomers loading things on to DC3s. The frantic, smoggy pace of Thailand seemed a world away.

The Shwe Dagon Pagoda, Rangoon

A little bus was there to take us across the tarmac, but it was easier to walk. Once inside, there was a small mêlée as queues attempted to form at wooden counters where immigration officials, each with a soldier at his side, were stamping passports and sweating. Fighting for space were Burmese in longyis, Thais in smart suits, American businessmen in reefer jackets and moustaches, a group of Japanese tourists in floppy hats and golf pants, a pink-faced priest in dog collar and black, and a couple of backpackers. One of these, an attractive Dutch woman, was wearing a T-shirt that said 'TINTIN IN THE CONGO'.

All up, we had filled half an A300, and the terminal was struggling to cope. Finally squeezing through the funnel, I was directed to the money exchange counter. When I'd got my visa in Bangkok I'd had to sign a declaration that said I would change US$200, not to be reconverted, on entering Burma. As I'd stood in line at the airport a young man had handed me a notice reminding me of this regulation, and the immigration officer had mentioned it again as he stamped my passport.

At the exchange counter, I signed two traveller's cheques and was given an envelope in return. I opened it and counted out 198 in crisp new Foreign Exchange Certificates (FEC), equivalent in value to the dollar, less one per cent commission. The paper had a design like the patterns we used to make with Spiro-Graph sets when we were kids, and no water mark. When I'd finished, I gave the clerk back the envelope. He said thanks and put it away carefully. I had passed Go.

As soon as I emerged from Customs there was a crowd of men in longyis asking me to change FEC or dollars, sell them cigarettes or whisky, or take their taxi — but preferably all five. I went with one of the cab drivers and, to forestall any more bargaining, pulled out a clump of kyats, which is only available to foreigners through the black market.

'Where did you get that?' the driver asked.

'I've been here before,' I said.

'Oh, so you must like Myanmar,' he said, trying to hide his disappointment.

'Yes, I like it very much.' And it's true. The Burmese are the kindest, sweetest-natured people you could hope to meet, and their country is beautiful. Where they got their government from, I will never know.

His vehicle was some kind of prehistoric Mazda, an odd Trabant-like thing painted blue. The rear compartment had open sides and back and two benches that looked as if they'd hold four schoolchildren each at a squeeze. I shoehorned myself into the cab with my knees up around my ears and my camera bag up against my chin, and shut the door with an unconvincing clunk.

Rangoon looked better without the dense canopy of monsoon cloud hanging over it which had made the city appear dark and mouldy on my first visit. The road was wide and smooth and there weren't many vehicles about, but those I saw were either similar to the one I was in, or quaint ramshackle Chevrolet buses that dated to the 1940s, or else white late model Japanese sedans. They were all right-hand drive, which wouldn't have seemed odd — this was, after all, a former British colony — except that we were driving on the right.

Downtown was a grid pattern of three and four-storey buildings with peeling plaster facades painted white, yellow or green, and the occasional gold-plated pagoda thrusting up blindingly bright in the sun. It looked much as I imagined most colonial capitals in Asia had looked like around World War II. The driver dropped me off at the Zar Chi Win Hotel, one of the few hotels in Rangoon open to foreigners, and I climbed the scungy staircase to the first floor. Inside, the hotel was an amazing bordello-like arrangement of canary-yellow walls, heavy lacquered wood and a lino floor. The rooms were about 2 metres (6½ feet) square, with masonite partitions for walls.

'How much?'

'Fifteen FEC. Or you can pay in dollars if you prefer,' said the manager.

I already knew that it was a government regulation that tourists had to pay for all accommodation, transport and official charges in foreign currency. First roll of the dice, and I'd landed on Old Kent Road with a hotel on it. I handed over my FEC.

'Would you like to change money?' asked a man who was lounging around the lobby.

'What's the rate?'

'For FEC, 105 kyats. For dollars, 110.' The official rate was 6 kyats to the dollar, which meant that if you changed money at the bank you were liable to go around paying for things at nearly twenty times their real value. And in the case of fares and accommodation, of course, you had to.

'That's less than when I was here last time. Has the dollar dropped?' It didn't seem all that likely that the kyat was rising.

'No,' he said. 'Mostly the money is used for the Chinese market, and the black market in China is now finished.'

I remembered that the yuan had been made convertible at the beginning of the year. For weeks afterwards, money changers had stood outside the hotels in Dali trying to induce tourists who hadn't heard the news to change money at a rate that was now less than what you could get in the bank. In the interest of honesty, I have to admit that I was one of their victims.

* * *

Next morning I called Jon Philp of the Australian Embassy, whom I had met on my first visit, to ask what he recommended I do to get permission to go to Bhamo. Jon gave me the name of a senior official in the Ministry, and told me that a group of foreign journalists had just been permitted to visit Myitkyina in the far north of the country, even further afield than Bhamo. This was encouraging news.

After trying repeatedly on the big black bakelite dial phone in the hotel, I finally got through on the number Jon had given me and found myself speaking to Htay Aung, a Director in the Ministry. I told him the long story of my efforts to get to Bhamo.

'First let me look into this,' he said. 'If you call again in half an hour I will try and find out what happened with your application.'

Half an hour later he told me that he hadn't been able to locate any trace of it. 'I suggest that you put in a new application and bring it here this afternoon. I will pass it on to the Minister and see what we can do.' I'd heard all this before, but there was something in his tone that was sympathetic. I went back to my room and wrote the letter.

When I'd finished I took it across to the Ministry building, which was just up the road. A soldier armed with a submachine gun at the entrance waved me through. Inside it seemed almost as gloomy as it had in the middle of monsoon, the fans wobbling lackadaisically overhead. I handed my application to a clerk who promised to pass it on, and emerged back into the glare.

Not far from the Ministry building is Scott Market, a large corrugated iron structure like a railway shed, built by the British. I walked over there in search of a new pair of runners to replace my old mountain boots, which I had originally bought in Kathmandu. They had taken me to Everest and back; they had been given emergency surgery in Chongqing by a roadside cobbler with a large hand-cranked stitching machine; they had been patched again in Kunming; and they had been brought back from the dead in Dali by a shoe repairer who was a genius in his way. But now they were beyond redemption.

I remembered Scott Market from my previous visit. Everyone I'd ever met who'd been to Burma had told me it was a land in isolation, where even basic consumer goods were not available, where people came up to you in the street to beg for pens, T-shirts, tampons, anything and everything they might need for everyday survival, and where the proceeds from a black market sale of a bottle of whisky and two cartons of cigarettes would keep you in spending money for the duration of your visa. Well, people still do ask you for all those things, and you can still sell whisky and Dunhills on the black market, but when I went to Scott Market I saw where it all ends up.

The road that surrounds it was jammed with white Nissans and Toyotas, honking their horns and moving at a snail's pace. Entering the market, I passed a couple of boutiques, a sign advertising Amway and a shop crammed with heavy metal paraphernalia. A group of young men with long hair, studded jackets and Iron Maiden badges hailed me as I walked past, and I waved back. A ghetto blaster

Scott Market, Rangoon

inside the shop was playing a cover of a Rod Stewart song, with lyrics in Burmese. It wasn't a bad rendition.

One wing of the market was devoted to food, and there I found everything from Vegemite to Pringles to corn flakes, to Lipton tea, Horlicks and Rose's lime cordial. There was Omo, Colgate and Wella Balsam, and Kraft processed cheddar cheese in blue tins; the inevitable Coke and Fanta and Seven Up; 555s and Marlboros and Lucky Strike, and VSOP and Gordon's gin and Johnnie Walker Red and Black. I found myself wishing I'd known about this place before I'd had my meeting with Myo Lwin.

There was a large section that sold only gold and jewellery, and then I got to the part where they sold clothes. Each stall was about 3 metres (10 feet) long, and raised above the ground on a platform; I found myself craning my neck to talk to a face that poked out from the middle of a thick curtain of merchandise.

'What you want? Levi? Lacoste? Reebok?'

'Let's have a look at some Reeboks.'

He pulled out some Reeboks that weren't really Reeboks, and then some Nikes that weren't really Nikes, and finally some Adidas that weren't really Adidas. They were all imports from Thailand, where the people have something of a gift for unlicensed imitations. They were about a quarter the price of the real thing, which still didn't make them all that cheap — about three times the Burmese average monthly wage, at a guess. The stallholder only had a couple of sizes of each, so I kept looking. Every stall on the block seemed to have the same stuff but in varying sizes. Finally I settled on some Coq Sportifs — the real thing, as far as I can tell, because I'm still wearing them — for US$40 and 5 FEC.

Who buys all this stuff, I asked myself. And then I answered: probably pretty much the same people who sell it — the smugglers, the army, the Chinese; anyone with enough connections to the government or the outside world to claw themselves up over the poverty line.

I left the carcasses of my boots on the footpath, thinking some street kid might find a use for them. I turned round thirty seconds later, and a teenage boy was inspecting them. When I looked again just before I turned the corner, he'd abandoned them in disdain.

Walking back to the hotel, I remembered the traders in Ruili and Tengchong with their jade and rubies, and the trucks loaded with timber, and I realised I had just seen the opposite side of the equation. From 1962 Burma had been ruled by a military regime that cut the country off from the outside world, more or less driving the economy into the ground. Then, in 1988, the people had risen in months of street demonstrations which only ended when the army intervened, butchering thousands in a massacre to rival Tiananmen Square (which happened a year later).

To solve the economic crisis the generals opted for an equally simple solution: they legitimised the black market and threw open their borders to trade. In exchange for their timber, gems, fish and rice, sold off at bargain basement prices to the Chinese and the Thais, they got the consumer goods they so desperately needed: things like padlocks, torches and stationery from China, and TV sets, secondhand Japanese cars and fake Reeboks from Thailand. The seal had been taken off the vacuum, and a weird sort of proto-capitalism had come rushing in. And so had something else: about one billion US dollars worth of new weapons from China, to be specific. The junta had bought itself a few more years.

Like the Chinese ten or fifteen years earlier, they were also discovering that inching open the door to tourists and making them buy Foreign Exchange Certificates was a handy way of earning much-needed foreign currency.

* * *

I called Htay Aung the next morning to ask if he'd got my application, and he told me to meet him that evening to discuss it. Then, with a sense of resigned inevitability, I went to look at the Shwe Dagon Pagoda. The Shwe Dagon is a bit like the Taj Mahal or the Sydney Opera House — if you go to Burma, sooner or later you're going to visit it. But the good thing about such mandatory sights — the Forbidden City, St Basil's, the Grand Canyon — is that they usually live up to expectations.

And in the middle of the run-down, ramshackle, crumbling colonial edifice that is Rangoon, the Shwe Dagon shines even brighter as an example of unadulterated magnificence, of radiant splendour, created for no better purpose than to bathe in its own brilliance. Burmese pagodas (which bear no resemblance to Chinese pagodas) are steep, conical affairs, a variant of the stupa, which originated in India as a shrine to house relics of the Buddha. The Shwe Dagon rises from a nest of scores of smaller pagodas. It is 98 metres (321 feet) high and plated with 8,688 slabs of solid gold, capped by a crown that contains 5,488 diamonds and 2,317 rubies, sapphires and topaz, and a huge emerald. Supposedly founded 2,500 years ago to house eight hairs from the Buddha's head, it is an exercise in sheer extravagance, the point being that material wealth itself is an illusion.

Devotees were kneeling in supplication, pouring libations on the statues that dotted the complex, or just walking round holding their children by the hand; I spotted a couple of Shan women in their indigo skirts and jackets and floppy headdresses, walking clockwise round the shrine. As I left I noticed a woman sitting patiently on the footpath outside, smoking a huge cigar as she waited for customers. At her feet were a number of small cages, each containing a bird. If you paid her some money, she would open the door to one of the cages and let the bird go free, and you would gain merit for your act of kindness to the creature. This ingenious example of private enterprise reminded me of something else I wanted to go and see, a sight that was definitely not on the tourist trail. I hailed a blue Mazda and asked the driver to take me to Inya Lake.

We drove through the leafy suburb of Golden Valley, home to diplomats and generals and one or two academics and doctors, the few remnants of Rangoon's élite who had not fled overseas after the military takeover. 'I lived in a pretty villa among noble trees on the lower slope of the hill which is crowned with the famous golden pagoda, the "Shway-dagon", the most sacred temple of Indo-China. We looked out upon the park and the royal lake,' wrote Morrison.

I got out at University Avenue and walked discreetly — as discreetly as a 6 foot 3 inches (190-centimetre) tall white man can walk in an Asian city — past the high-walled villa that had been pointed out to me by a friend on my earlier visit. Inside was a rather delicate-looking academic who was also, incidentally, a Nobel laureate and the elected leader of the country. I didn't see her, but I knew she was there.

Aung San Suu Kyi's main claim to fame when she returned to the family villa from her home in England to nurse her ailing mother in 1988 was that her father was the immensely popular general who had led Burma to the brink of inde-pendence, only to be assassinated before he could take office as leader. That she returned just as the country was exploding with anti-government demonstrations

Rangoon

was, it seems, a coincidence. But when the military the next year announced it was going to allow elections, she immediately became the focus of the campaign. In the poll, her party, the National League for Democracy, scored sixty per cent of the vote, taking 392 out of 485 contested seats. The army's party got about twenty per cent.

Go to jail. Go directly to jail. Do not pass Go. Do not collect $200.

When I visited Rangoon in September 1993, there had been four clumsily built sentry posts in front of the house, each with a couple of soldiers toting semi-automatic weapons. But this time around the sentry posts had disappeared, leaving nothing to distinguish the house from the other comfortable mansions that lined the shores of the lake. It was hard to tell what this signified, but I wasn't about to try for a closer look.

Back downtown I sought out the Indian quarter, where the remnants of the community brought over by the British to serve as everything from labourers to traders to clerks and doctors still lived — most of them had also fled persecution in the sixties — and stuffed my belly to bursting with rice and curry served on a banana leaf. This served the desired purpose of bringing on a siesta, after which it was time for my appointment at the Ministry.

I waited for about an hour in the now nearly deserted building before Htay Aung emerged. He came out of the Minister's office, which was through a door sectioned off by a curtain, giving the impression he'd just been in audience with a Bedouin sheik. He was carrying my application, which I noticed now had a large stamp and a signature on it. He was wearing a longyi and a button-across Chinese-style jacket, the local equivalent of a lounge suit. Like many Burmese men, he looked younger than I had expected.

We hummed and hawed for about a quarter of an hour in his office. I explained who I was and what I wanted to do and why I wanted to get to Bhamo. I told him about Morrison, but it was obvious he wasn't very interested in Morrison. He was interested in my money.

'Your application has been approved by the Minister,' he told me. 'But now it must go to the Defence Department for approval, and to the SLORC. This will take some time.'

'I don't have much time. I must be back in Australia in two weeks.'

'This will be difficult, but I will try. Are you willing to take a package tour?'

'Yes, if you think that will make it easier,' I said, swallowing the bait.

'Alright, let's go downstairs and organise a package tour,' he said, a bit too quickly.

I followed him down the creaking stairs to another cavernous room where I was introduced to another official. Htay Aung said something to him in Burmese and left us.

The man began looking up flight schedules and prices in big books that he pulled from under his desk and drew a list of figures on a pad. 'You must go with an official guide,' he said when he had finished. 'The charge for the guide is US$50 per day. You can fly from Rangoon to Bhamo, spend two days at Bhamo, then fly to Myitkyina, four nights in Myitkyina, fly to Mandalay, then return to Rangoon by train as you like.'

All up, US$890. I would have to pay the guide's fares in foreign currency as well as my own. I almost laughed. More than 1,000 Australian for what might well turn out to be a few days in dusty military camps? No thanks. I went back upstairs to talk to Htay Aung.

We reached a compromise. I would catch the train up to Mandalay, which is as far north as foreign tourists are normally permitted to go. A guide would be provided in Mandalay, and I would fly with him to Bhamo. Then I could take the riverboat back to Mandalay. The whole itinerary was typed out in triplicate in the curly Burmese script, sealed and signed and a copy given to me to present to the Myanmar Travels and Tours office in Mandalay. I shook hands with Htay Aung and thanked him; he was just doing his job, and he was doing it better than some.

Then I went downstairs and bought a train ticket for Mandalay for the next morning. The real price was written on the front: 171 kyats, which was just a bit more than the price of my curry lunch. I handed over my $35 and got out of there.

* * *

The train from Rangoon to Mandalay takes about sixteen hours if you don't get a derailment along the way. The carriages are comfortable, shiny new ones made in South Korea, but the tracks date back to British times.

The train lurched at something like 30 kilometres (19 miles) an hour along the ancient line and dawn gradually bloomed across a scene of low hills and paddy fields and straw huts and pagodas and labouring buffalo. There was something odd about this landscape, which at first I couldn't quite put my finger on. And then I had it: the lack of people. Well, there *were* people, bending in the fields or sitting in the rattletrap trucks that chug-chugged along the roads, but there weren't enough of them. Burma is the same size as Texas, yet its population is only forty million which, compared with its neighbours, makes it relatively unpopulated. Earlier this century, it was one of the world's major rice exporters. Now it is officially ranked by the UN as one of the ten poorest countries.

For days, something had been bugging me, some parallel that I knew was there. Now I realised what it was. The abundance of natural wealth, the discount sell-off of resources, the back-to-front infrastructure, the easygoing, unambitious people — Burma was a bit like my own country. Australia, but with hill tribes and hunger and a civil war.

Across the aisle was an old monk in burgundy robes smoking Dunhills from a packet he kept stashed in one of the folds, and in the seat next to me was a young man who turned out to be a soldier. He had a friendly, engaging manner, but his limited English and my even more limited Burmese confined us to exchanging the usual politenesses and banalities before lapsing back into silence. As the journey wore on, he produced a bottle of evil-smelling white spirits, which he proceeded to drink through a pink straw. He offered me a swig but I declined. As the booze slipped down his throat, it oiled his tongue.

He was rejoining his unit in Myitkyina — pronounced *Mitchina* — the headquarters of the North-Eastern Command and the capital of Kachin State. From this remote and malarial station, the war against the Kachin Independence Army had been sputtering on for more than thirty years.

'Do you like Myitkyina?' I asked him.

'No,' he said. 'It is dirty. The people are dirty. I do not like their way.'

'Their way?'

'Free sex,' he said as an explanation. Then I remembered this rather colourful detail about the Kachin: that there are apparently no restrictions on premarital sex. Amateur anthropologists of the British colonial administration, who did the first scientific studies of Burma's hill people, had usually noted it with restrained glee.

'I don't like this free sex. I don't like these people,' said the soldier. His friendly features twisted into a grimace that wasn't entirely a product of the alcohol, and I got my first inkling of the complexities and ethnic rivalries that have turned the history of independent Burma into such a sad chronicle of repression and bloodshed.

'I am Karen — we are Christian. We do not believe in free sex,' he added.

This surprised me. I had assumed he was a Burman, a member of the Buddhist plains-dwelling majority who dominate the army and the government. The Karen are another minority like the Kachin. Based near the Thai border until recently, they too have waged a long and bitter struggle for independence against the Burman-dominated state. Many of them are Baptists, converted by American missionaries during the colonial period. But then, so are many of the Kachin. And still they can't get together to win the war.

'Next year I will go Singapore. I will work — as ship sailor or other thing,' said the soldier, naming one of the few avenues of escape from Burma's economic deprivations. 'My family is poor. We have not a car.'

'How much are you paid?' I asked him.

'I am army accountant. My salary is 1,500 kyats per month. Senior general is paid 2,500 kyats per month.' At the unofficial exchange rate, that came to less than US$25.

'Will the government let you go?' I asked.

'I don't know. Government is not ...' — and this time he leaned so close to whisper that I could almost taste the fumes on his breath — '... good.' Soon afterwards he collapsed into a stupor, his mouth a red slash of betel like a fresh wound. With even soldiers whispering dissent, it wasn't surprising that the government was having trouble beating the insurgents. The train rumbled on towards Mandalay.

Buddhist nuns, Rangoon

中国

Market scene, Rangoon

Buddhist nuns collect alms in the early morning, Bhamo

Mandalay Palace

Market, Bhamo

Far from being the city of romance immortalised by Kipling, Mandalay is a dusty sprawl of wide treeless streets and low grey buildings. The main places of interest lie outside it: the kings of Upper Burma had a habit of shifting capitals, so Mandalay is surrounded by the skeletons of cities with wonderful names like Ava and Sagaing and Amarapura. But the modern town was built by the British, and its grid-pattern streets suggest a tropical version of one of the less interesting suburbs of Melbourne. I can't imagine that anyone has ever written a song about the road to Moorabbin, but Mandalay does have a tram line. I never did see a tram on it.

River traffic on the Irrawaddy

CHAPTER TWELVE

SLOW BOAT TO MANDALAY

Mandalay and Bhamo

Instead, there are hundreds of rickshaws. Every Asian country has its variant on the original cycle rickshaw designed by the Japanese last century, and in Burma it consists of a bicycle with a sidecar, one seat facing forwards and the other backwards. If you overload the rear seat, the whole thing is liable to up-end like a dragster and veer out of control into the nearest gutter, as I discovered once to the amusement of everyone in sight. This one was taking me to the tourist office at the Mandalay Hotel.

As we treadled along the uniform streets, I noticed a lot of new buildings going up: large houses and places that looked as if they might end up as hotels or department stores. Some of them had satellite dishes on their roofs. There had been a bit of this going on in Rangoon too, but not as much.

'Who is building all these new houses?' I asked the rickshaw man.

'Oh, that is Chinese people,' he told me. 'Many of them come to Mandalay now. It is easy for them. They have a lot of money. They just pay to army, and army say OK. Many Chinese people in Mandalay now. House is getting very expensive.'

'Chinese people from China, or from other parts of Myanmar?'

'Some come from China. They bring things from China and sell. Others, they sell — what you call it? — medicine.'

'Drugs? You mean, heroin?'

'Yes, that one. We call it medicine. They bring it here, then they take it to Thailand or India. One man, one time he ask me to take some kilos to Thailand for him. He said he will pay me 40,000 kyats. So much money, no?'

Forty thousand kyats is less than US$400.

I had heard stories like this on my last visit, too, from people I can't name. When the old Communist Party collapsed up in the Golden Triangle, the government had quietly allowed some of the opium barons to come and set up shop in Mandalay. The army gained their allegiance, while the dealers got a chance to leave the festering jungle and make a solid investment in real estate. The trade continued much as before. As well as the drugs trade, Mandalay is the distribution point for the legitimate cross-border trade from Yunnan. China's boom had spilled across the border and was transforming Mandalay from a sleepy town of half a million or so into Burma's most important commercial centre.

'What do you think of the Chinese people?' I asked my friend.

'I don't like. Now Mandalay belong Chinese people. Burmese people cannot afford to live in the city any more.'

'Mandalay is largely Chinese,' wrote Morrison, later quoting an authority on Burma, J.G. Scott, who said that 'the plodding, unwearying Chinaman is almost certainly destined to overrun the country to the exclusion of the native race.'

Village scene at dusk on the Irrawaddy

River boat on the Irrawaddy

Soldiers on the Irrawaddy river boat

Passengers, Irrawaddy river boat

We had arrived at the Mandalay Hotel, opposite the vast 2-kilometre (1¼-mile) square moated and walled Royal Palace, once home to King Thibaw, the last ruler of Upper Burma before the British relieved him of his duties in 1885. The British toyed with the idea of demolishing the complex to demonstrate that they were there to stay, but finally opted for a subtler approach: they renamed it Fort Dufferin and made it the headquarters of their administration in Upper Burma, turning its elaborate audience halls, pavilions and royal chambers of lacquered teak into official residences, offices, a church and a club; Morrison spent hours here catching up on the papers on his way down from Bhamo.

The Japanese used the compound as a military camp, and were still holding out there in March 1945 when the British arrived to retake it. The palace was shelled and bombed, and every stick of teak down to the last baroque detail evaporated in a storm of fire. The only things left standing were the stout stone walls.

Nowadays much of the area is once again a military camp but, in the middle, the palace is being rebuilt for the sake of the tourist trade — for US$5 you can go inside and look at some scaffolding and some half-finished pavilions. By the main gate there is a military checkpost and a big red sign with white letters that reads, in Burmese and English, 'THE TATMADAW [Army/Government] SHALL NEVER BETRAY THE NATIONAL CAUSE.' Or at least there was then. By now the English part of it may have been painted over, leaving only the Burmese; this had happened to similar billboards I'd seen in Rangoon.

I paid the rickshaw man, and he pleaded with me to hire him for the duration of my stay, to allow him to show me the sights of Mandalay. 'I don't think I will have time,' I said.

'You want to go to antique shop? Restaurant? Change money? I will wait for you.' And, sure enough, when I emerged some hours later, he was still there, along with about a dozen others.

My itinerary sent the manager at the MTT office into a minor panic. He got straight on the phone to Rangoon to triple-check the authorisation and then, satisfied, arranged my flight to Bhamo. There were only two flights a week, and a couple of passengers had to be bumped, which made me feel a bit guilty. He also arranged for a guide, who turned up an hour or two later. He had on a longyi and a collared shirt, and introduced himself as Ronald. Like most Burmese, he had a bit of a smile the whole time.

'Have you been to Bhamo before?' I asked him.

'Yes. In 1992 I went there with Mr Klein, an Austrian man who was writing a guidebook. That time we were accompanied by an officer from the Military Intelligence Department in Rangoon, and by six soldiers armed with Uzi submachine guns.' This time around, I was glad to hear, it was just going to be Ronald and me.

We spent the next morning sitting in the drab, empty, whitewashed building that is Mandalay Airport. Finally, around one-thirty, a bullet-bodied little Fokker buzzed in out of the sky and bumped along the runway, and soon we were walking across the baking tarmac and in up under the tail. I'm normally a pretty calm flier, but I have to admit that this time I was worried. This thing was thirty years old if it was a day. The windows were so scratched and grimy you could barely see through them, the interior finish was cracked and stained, and the entire cabin stank. The fuselage shook as we gathered speed for take-off, and a couple of overhead lockers sprang open.

From the air, Mandalay looked like a big brown and green chessboard, the white pagodas marching like pawns across its regular face. Lying at the edge of it was the huge square of the palace. I pondered the fact that its every occupant for the last 100 years had ended up being comprehensively checkmated — except the Tatmadaw, that is, who sat there now, oiling their new Chinese AK-47s. Then there were khaki patchwork fields and the occasional cluster of huts, the big languid bends of the Irrawaddy, and then the mountains and the bush took over and humanity disappeared from sight.

After forty-five minutes we touched down on a short and very bumpy runway. There was a crowd of military personnel on the tarmac and a number of jeeps surrounding the plane, each with a black heavy machine gun manned by a soldier in a bush hat. The guns, I was relieved to note, were pointing away from the plane.

Ronald smiled at my discomfiture. 'This is a precaution in case the Kachins attack the aircraft,' he said. 'But don't worry, that won't happen. If there was any chance of that, you wouldn't be here.'

Under one wing was the cargo van, a jalopy of a truck with huge flapping mudguards, a crankhole in the bumper bar and a bunch of spinach, presumably the driver's dinner, draped over one of the headlamps. I tried hard to identify it, but all its badges had disappeared. It looked as though it dated from about 1930. Ronald had to do some explaining about me at the terminal, and then we joined the city transfer, which turned out to be the same vehicle. I got pride of place in the front as we wheezed and jolted the couple of kilometres into Bhamo.

The town was mostly solid-looking teak buildings the colour that old chocolate goes as it turns to powder, standing on stilts the thickness of elephants' legs, with paling fences and yards sprouting with jungle and big pink flowers. The place looked much as I imagined it would have done 100 years ago, but a single match could change all that in a matter of minutes. Rutted roads led this way and that and the whole town had the snoozy feel that Orwell captured so well in his fine, bitter first novel, *Burmese Days*. Entering the outskirts, we passed a Christian cemetery, the white crosses wilting with neglect, and I thought of boredom and billiards and whisky on the verandah and Henrietta, and the little ones back in Hampshire being told that poor Archie had succumbed to fever in Bhamo and not quite understanding what it had all been for, or where exactly Bhamo was, for that matter. Later, I discovered the cemetery was for Burmese Christians.

In a few minutes we were in the centre of town and taking a room at a hotel. They'd never heard of FEC here, and the rooms were 100 kyats each — one for me and one for Ronald. I'd hit Free Parking at last. I washed my face and then we went down to the local MTT office to sort out my itinerary. Ronald introduced me to his local counterpart, a jolly, short, round fellow called Ki Maung Than. I found his Christian name easier to deal with: it was Angus. He was half Baptist and half Catholic, he told me, and had studied at a Christian school in Rangoon — as had Ronald.

Angus seemed a bit bored. His main duty in Bhamo was to make arrangements for the occasional group of Chinese tourists who came across the border. 'In Rangoon or Mandalay, we get to take Japanese groups around, and they always give us very good tips. But here, you can't make any money. Our salary is barely enough to survive on.' Ronald told me his salary was 1,200 kyats a month. He spoke excellent English and French, and had a degree from Rangoon University.

I left them to it and went for a walk. People waved and smiled shyly at me from their balconies, and giggled uncontrollably whenever I produced a camera. As in Mandalay and Rangoon, the women had plastered their cheeks with the yellow paste called *thanaka*, made from bark, to protect their skin from the sun. Some of them smoked large cheroots wrapped in green leaves.

I walked down to the Irrawaddy, here a broad green strip sparkling its way through a field of pale sand. A couple of boys in shorts were wrestling and laughing, and over by the water a family was fixing a boat. None of them paid me any attention. The afternoon light was as clear and brassy as a temple bell, and I could sense the silence of the jungle on the nearby hills. I sat for a few minutes on the sand and thought over and over again, *I've done it*. I shut out the fact that this meant that in a week and a half I would be returning to Sydney.

I went back to the travel office, which was actually just a meeting room of the local Chinese community centre. There was also a temple and a restaurant in the centre, and a banquet was in full swing out in the open air. Ronald told me that there had been a wedding, and that we were all invited to join the meal. We sat down to a table groaning with food: eggs in pork, pork in eggs, preserved eggs, pickled vegetables, fried peanuts, more pork, and clear rice liquor. By this time I'd abandoned any pretence at vegetarianism, and dug in.

Ronald had been telling everyone that I had just been in China, and people crowded around, smiling, to speak to me. They spoke Chinese with thick accents, and I told them of my adventures in laboured sentences, Ronald translating into Burmese whenever the going got tough. We toasted each other, my hosts filled my plate to overflowing and we toasted each other again with that fearsome alcohol. According to Ronald, the Chinese made up about one quarter of the population of Bhamo, many of the families having fled across the border during the Muslim rebellion over 100 years ago. Now they controlled much of the town's commerce.

The bride and groom came to greet us, she in red and he in a double-breasted suit; we shook hands and I took the two cigarettes that the groom proffered and put them in my pocket. Chinese New Year was only a few days away, and Ronald told me that the next year would be inauspicious for weddings, so a lot had been scheduled for the next few days. Next day we had the leftovers for lunch, and the following night we joined another banquet.

One of the Chinese businessmen kindly offered me the use of his car to explore the town, and the next morning I set off with Ronald and Angus and a driver.

> The finest residence in Bhamo is, of course, the American mission. America nobly supports her self-sacrificing and devoted sons who go forth to arrest the 'awful ruin of souls' among the innumerable millions of Asia, who are 'perishing without hope, having sinned without law'. The missionary in charge told me that he labours with a 'humble heart to bring a knowledge of the Saving Truth to the perishing heathen among the Kachins'.

The head of the mission was a man named William Henry Roberts. God had come to Roberts, who was a native of Virginia, during a particularly pressing moment of the American Civil War, I read in the mission records. Roberts told God that he would do whatever God commanded if he made it off the battlefield alive. God took him at his word, commanding him to go to Bhamo to convert the heathen.

The first Baptist missionary to set his sights on Bhamo was a man called Albert J. Lyon, who arrived in February 1878. Within a week he had contracted malaria, and a month later he was dead. Roberts arrived in 1879, via Mandalay, where he was granted land for the mission in an audience with King Thibaw. He stayed until 1913.

We pulled up outside a rambling compound on the outskirts of town and got out. In front of us was a squat, slightly bizarre pile of river rocks: the Roberts Memorial Church, built in 1938. As we left the grounds, a neat-looking man in a longyi and suit jacket came up and introduced himself as Paul Naw Taung, the pastor of the Bhamo Baptist Mission. He showed us around the mission and as we talked I asked him if any of the buildings dated to Roberts's time.

Kachin woman, Bhamo

'Yes, Roberts built many of these buildings himself. This one was his house,' he said, gesturing to a solid wooden building with stilts and a corrugated iron roof. The Reverend pointed out to me a number of marks in the massive teak supports where he said Japanese bullets had slapped into it in World War II. Parked beside it was the mission vehicle — an American jeep of the same vintage. I felt for a moment as if time had stood still, much as I had in the Mekong gorge. We went inside; the rooms were large, cool and airy. It seemed likely that in 1894 it had indeed been the finest residence in Bhamo. Where an Englishman would have put in a cottage and a rose garden, the Virginian had built himself a top-of-the-line log cabin.

Later in the day we returned to take tea with the Reverend. The sky had darkened, and the clouds burst just as we arrived. Upstairs in his house — another cool, woody haven — Mrs Naw Taung gave us bright yellow Madeira cake and sweet, milky, Indian-style tea, and I leafed through some mission records that the pastor had dug out for me. I asked him how the mission had fared since the departure of the vigorous Mr Roberts. Paul told me that the Bhamo District Baptist Association, of which he was secretary, currently had twenty-nine churches and about 10,000 baptised members.

'Are the members mostly Kachin, or Burman?'

'Among our members are Kachin, Karen, Shan, Lesu and Chinese. There are only two Burmese families who have converted.'

'So most of the converts are Kachin?'

'Yes. I myself am a Kachin.'

'Are there many Catholics in the area?' Earlier that day we had visited a large, colourful, deserted Catholic church.

'Not as many as there are Baptists. The Catholic missionaries arrived here first, but the Baptists have been far more successful.'

'Why do you think that is?'

'You see, the Kachin are a very independent-minded people. For centuries they have been their own masters, up here in the jungle. They will never put up with the Pope telling them what to do. So you see, the Baptist Church suits us much better.'

'Are there many Kachin Baptists on the Chinese side of the border?'

'There used to be until the 1960s. But then those people were persecuted. I don't know what is happening there now.'

'Are you still getting converts?'

'Oh yes. Each year I baptise about 200 people. I baptise them here in the Irrawaddy, 100 at a time.'

'I understand that many of the Kachin mix their old animist beliefs with Christianity.'

'No, nobody does that. But there are about eighty families left who still practise animism.'

'Do American missionaries still come here?'

'No. The last American missionary left in the 1960s. At that time our school was also nationalised. We used to run a primary and a middle school with about 800 pupils, but now it is a government school.' I had seen the school in the morning, its big open windows crowded with laughing faces goggling at the foreigner.

Ronald told me later that most foreign missionaries had been expelled from Burma during the 1960s because it was suspected they were helping to foment various tribal insurgencies. According to Bertil Lintner, one of the reasons the Kachin had rebelled — and they were among the last of the various ethnic groups to do so — was that in 1961 Buddhism had been proclaimed the sole state religion. This was seen as another example of Burman arrogance, the last in a string of provocations from Rangoon.*

'Do you also minister to the Kachins in the mountains?' I asked Paul.

'I serve all Baptists in this area. I have been to the mountain areas, yes.' He shot a quick glance at the guides. We were straying on to dangerous territory, which in Burma is never very far away. Outside, the rain had stopped. I asked the Reverend if I could borrow his books to look through that night, and we left.

Just next door to the mission, on a separate block of land, was another church, a tall, pale-yellow bell tower fronting a simple wood building. I asked Angus what kind of church it was.

'That is the church of the Karen Baptists,' he said.

There was one other place Morrison had described that I wanted to see: the fort to which the British, having handed out a few warnings against interfering with the cross-border trade, then sensibly withdrew, leaving the Kachin to their own devices and the attentions of the missionaries. I asked Ronald if he knew where it was.

'That place is now the army camp,' he said.

'Can we go there, tomorrow perhaps?'

'We can try.' But something in his voice told me he thought it wasn't such a good idea.

This brings me to the matter of the country's name, which was officially changed in May 1990. The word 'Burma' is a British corruption of Myanmar, the traditional name for the people of the Irrawaddy Valley — a fairly standard example of colonial pronunciation. A number of cities have also reverted to their old names, including Rangoon, which is now officially Yangon.

Although widely used by the Burman majority, the term 'Myanmar' doesn't embrace the mountains that surround the central plain — in other words, it excludes the minorities, who make up over thirty per cent of the country's population. If 'Burma' recalls imperial indifference, then 'Myanmar' suggests Burman chauvinism. British rule might not have been the most attractive spectacle, but it's long gone. Until somebody comes up with something better, I'm sticking with 'Burma'.

Children, Mandalay

On the way back we passed a sign which said, 'ANYONE WHO GETS RIOTOUS, DESTRUCTIVE AND UNRULY IS OUR ENEMY.'

I spent the next day wandering around Bhamo at my own pace. I had hoped to take a run out to the Chinese border in the car, but this wasn't possible. A road runs about halfway to the point where Morrison crossed, Ronald told me, and then peters out in the jungle. The border itself is controlled by the Kachin Independence Army.

So instead I went out at dawn and visited the market, more monasteries, the cemetery and what someone told me was once the residence of the British Deputy Commissioner, where Morrison stayed — it's now a government guest house — and then I went back to the mission to return Paul's books to him. Often people waved to me as they passed on bicycles, and I heard them say to each other, 'Australia'.

That evening, as Ronald and Angus and I ate a dinner of river prawns and fried noodles washed down by Mandalay beer and local rum, I tried to tell them about my day.

'We know exactly where you have been,' said Ronald with a smile. 'You have been to the market and the cemetery and the guest house and the mission.'

I guess I looked perplexed.

'We have been at the office all day,' he explained. 'The phone must have rung at least ten times. It was the Intelligence Department. They were very worried that you might try and go outside town, or near the army camp. They were trying to follow you, but you were walking too fast. They couldn't keep up! They kept asking me where you were going next. I said to them, how would I know!'

* * *

Before dawn next morning we were up and in a tonga taking us to the landing station on the river. There, Ronald and I embarked on a large white double-decker passenger-and-cargo riverboat.

'In a steamer of the Irrawaddy Flotilla Company I came down the river from Bhamo to Mandalay,' wrote Morrison; as the river unfolded before my eyes, I could hardly believe that he'd devoted just one sentence of his entire book to this gorgeous, 400-kilometre (248-mile) stretch of water. But now I can see why. Those three days have coalesced in my mind into a bliss of jungle-coated ridges and villages on stilts. The boat glided downstream, stopping at tiny villages where men and women would labour for hours loading and unloading the produce of Upper Burma — reed mats, sticks, bamboo, dried fish, grimy and battered drums of cooking oil — up groaning gangplanks or off wobbling canoes. I remember monks and fisherfolk, and bullock carts creaking along the banks; blue skies ribbed with high cloud, golden sand and green water and ancient launches towing wide flotillas of teak down to Mandalay; papaya and pineapple and sugar bananas; thatched roofs and straw hats; villagers laughing and bathing at dusk in water of smoky cyan, and then dawn over the empty river like a late Turner; soldiers and babies and marathon card games; tea with condensed milk, and cheroots, and oily fish curry; rafts and palm trees and peeling pagodas winking white in the sun, and only the steady chog-chog-chog of the diesels to remind me that this was 1994, not 1894. I read, wrote and took photos, talked to Ronald, dozed, soaked up the sun in a deckchair, and wallowed in the exhaustion of five and a half months of non-stop travel. At last I understood what Kipling had meant. It wasn't Mandalay he was talking about. It's how you get there.

In Mandalay I said goodbye to Ronald, and pressed some FEC into his hand. It was an awkward moment for both of us, but he took it. I caught the overnight train to Rangoon, and a day or two later I was in Bangkok, and a day or two after that I was in a plane slicing its way through the wide sky towards Australia. From Rangoon Morrison had sailed to Calcutta, where he promptly collapsed with remittent fever and almost died, not for the first or last time in his life. As soon as he was well enough, he accelerated his convalescence by having an affair with his nurse.

I got on the plane at Bangkok Airport on the evening of 11th February 1994 with a bunch of Aussies brown from the sun of Phuket. One hundred years before, to the day, Morrison had stood in his Chinese outfit on the deck of the Jardine Matheson steamer as it eased its way up the Huangpu heading for Wuhan.

A couple of weeks later I read in the newspapers that, after thirty-three years of fighting, the Kachin Independence Organisation had signed a ceasefire agreement with the SLORC.

Perhaps if I'd left Shanghai in February 1994 instead of September 1993, by the time I got to the Burmese border the government would have allowed me to cross as Morrison had.

Probably not, but perhaps.

EPILOGUE

I noted early in the book that the accuracy of some of Morrison's reporting for *The Times* during his years in Peking has been called into question, and that this allegation touches on issues as fundamental as the very way in which China is perceived by the West. Serious charges have been made, and they deserve to be addressed seriously. However, an objective appraisal of Morrison's career has yet to appear in English. Cyril Pearl's book is little more than hagiography, bulked out with voluminous excerpts from Morrison's own accounts. Sterling Seagrave, on the other hand, in his worthy effort to un-demonise Cixi, the Empress Dowager, has unfortunately been tempted into the convenient strategy of demonising Morrison to strengthen his argument.

Mine has been a travel book, and an exploration of Morrison's later career, involving as it does a quarter of a century of intrigue among half a dozen empires, is obviously way beyond its scope. But for someone with a few languages and a decade or two to spare, there is a fascinating PhD thesis to be written, starting with the 300-odd books and boxes of the Morrison Collection in the Mitchell Library in Sydney.

I have only concerned myself here with Morrison's account of his journey across China. *An Australian in China* carries a significant imperialist bias, although this is generally not more or less pronounced than the writings of other Western visitors to China at the time. It was, after all, 1894. Otherwise, as far as was possible, given the 100 years of turmoil that intervene, I found Morrison's descriptions of scenes and encounters along the route to be closely observed and precise. If he later used his position to promote a cause which, with hindsight, appears distasteful and tragic, this does not detract from his achievements as a pioneer of Western reporting on Asian affairs.

But I have found one bit of evidence about that book which intrigues me. Some time after returning to Australia, I was sitting in the airy Special Collections Room of the Mitchell Library looking through the drafts and proofs of *An Australian in China*. Instead of the yells and smells and crush of Asia, I was surrounded by stained glass, polished wood and the muted shuffles of scholars poring.

At the end of the volume are two pages of handwritten notes. The first of these appears to be a list of changes suggested by an authority on China to whom the book had been referred. The suggestions imply a number of factual errors in the book. They are not major errors, and their correction wouldn't have involved more than a few small adjustments to the text. But Morrison didn't bother with them. One of the suggestions refers to the following passage:

> At the poor old shrine to the God of Riches, half a dozen Chinamen in need of the god's good offices were holding a small feast in his honour. They had prepared many dishes and, having 'dedicated to the god the spiritual essence, were now about to partake of the insipid remains'. 'Ching fan', they courteously said to us when we approached down the path.

'Did the Chinese say *Ching fan?*' asks the anonymous expert. 'They ought to have said *Ch'ing chih fan* but sometimes people are in a hurry.'*

There is more evidence of a man in a hurry on the next page. This time the notes are in Morrison's writing. Apparently written before the book was published, they seem to be a list of the new author's aims and achievements at the turning point of his life. They make interesting reading.

1. Book to be a great success.
2. To enable me to pay up my debts.
3. To enable me to telegraph out, 'Book published by Macmillan or other great success'.
4. News of victory in Summer Cup or money. [crossed out]
5. Many new photographs sent me.
6. Book all ready without effort.
7. Every assistance given in time of need.
8. Abundance of money forthcoming.
9. My portrait in the PMB. [crossed out]
10. Big rise in South Seas. [crossed out]
11. All well and flourishing at home.
12. Uninterrupted good fortune in London &c.
13. To become a great newspaper correspondent.
14. To go back to New Guinea.
15. The Medal of the Royal Humane Society.

---

* This authority also notes that the picture titled 'Opium smoking' in Morrison's book — which appears here on page 146 — is 'evidently a got-up one — the 2 men are not opium smoking — at least, the one with the shoes on is not — & the photo is altogether confused & confusing'.

16. To have won Cup money by wager (cf 10) much money.
17. That I may be instrumental in bringing about war over the Far East and be famous the world over.

I can't think of any better words than these to sum up the ambitious, obsessive, gifted, egotistical, energetic, callous, romantic, ironic, complex, contradictory man that was George Ernest Morrison as he stood on the threshold of what is sometimes called greatness. As usual, he'd beaten me to it.

MORRISON'S ROUTE IN 1894

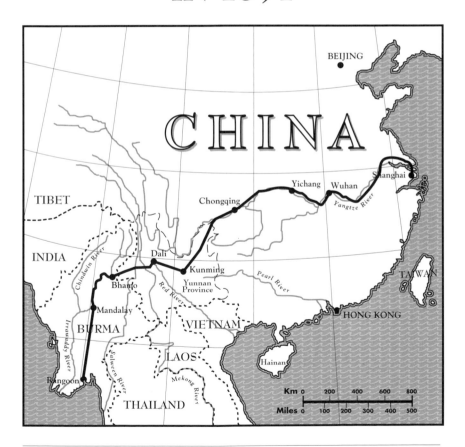

BIBLIOGRAPHY

This list includes works of fiction, travel, academic and general interest; it is intended simply as a starting point for anyone who may wish to pursue some of the areas touched upon by this book.

CHAPTER ONE

Immanuel C.Y. Hsu, *The Rise of Modern China* (4th edition, Oxford University Press, New York, 1990).

Lo Hui-min (ed.), *The Correspondence of G.E. Morrison* (Cambridge University Press, 1978).

G.E. Morrison, *An Australian in China* (Horace Cox, London, 1895).

Joseph Needham, *Science and Civilisation in China* (Cambridge University Press, 1988).

Cyril Pearl, *Morrison of Peking* (Angus & Robertson, Sydney, 1967).

Sterling Seagrave, *Dragon Lady: The Life and Legend of the Last Empress of China* (Macmillan, London, 1992).

H.R. Trevor-Roper, *Hermit of Peking: The Hidden Life of Sir Edmund Backhouse* (Knopf, New York, 1977).

CHAPTER TWO

Noel Barber, *The Fall of Shanghai: The Communist Take-over in 1949* (Macmillan, London, 1979).

Nicholas R. Clifford, *Spoilt Children of the Empire: Westerners in Shanghai and the Chinese Revolution of the 1920s* (Middlebury College Press, Vermont, 1991).

Pan Ling, *In Search of Old Shanghai* (Joint Publishing, Hong Kong, 1982).

CHAPTERS THREE, FOUR AND FIVE

Margaret Barber and Grainne Ryder (eds.), *Damming the Three Gorges* (2nd edition, Earthscan, London and Toronto, 1993).

Han Suyin, *Destination Chungking* (Cape, London, 1943).

Lyman, P. van Slyke, *Yangtze: Nature, History and the River* (Addison Wesley, Reading, Mass., 1988).

CHAPTERS SIX, SEVEN, EIGHT AND NINE

John Anderson, *Mandalay to Momien: A Narrative of the Two Expeditions to Western China of 1868 and 1875* (Macmillan, London, 1876).

Charles Backus, *The Nan-chao Kingdom and T'ang China's Southwestern Frontier* (Cambridge University Press, Cambridge and New York, 1981).

C.P. Fitzgerald, *The Tower of Five Glories: A Study of the Min Chia of Ta Li* (Cresset Press, London, 1941).

— *The Southern Expansion of the Chinese People: 'Southern Fields and Southern Ocean'* (ANU Press, Canberra, 1972).

Werner Forman, *The Travels of Marco Polo* (Michael Joseph, London, 1971).

Dru C. Gladney, *Muslim Chinese: Ethnic Nationalism in the People's Republic* (Council on East Asian Studies, Harvard University, Cambridge, Mass. and London, 1965).

T.R. Tregear, *A Geography of China* (University of London Press, London, 1965).

Barbara W. Tuchman, *Stilwell and the American Experience in China, 1911–45* (Macmillan, New York, 1970).

CHAPTER TEN

John King Fairbank (ed.), *The Missionary Enterprise in China and America* (Harvard University Press, Mass., 1974).

J.C.S. Hall, *Yunnan Provincial Faction 1927–1937* (Department of Far Eastern History, ANU, Canberra, 1976).

Kenneth Scott Latourette, *A History of Christian Missions in China* (Russell & Russell, London, 1929).

Alfred W. McCoy, *The Politics of Heroin: CIA Complicity in the Global Drugs Trade* (Lawrence Hill Books, New York, 1991).

Royal Commission on Opium (British Government, London, 1894–95).

CHAPTERS ELEVEN AND TWELVE

E.C.V. Foucar, *Mandalay the Golden* (Dobson, London, 1963).

Bertil Lintner, *Land of Jade: A Journey through Insurgent Burma* (Kiscadale, Edinburgh and White Lotus, Bangkok, 1990).

— *Outrage: Burma's Struggle for Democracy* (White Lotus, Bangkok, 1990).

George Orwell, *Burmese Days* (Secker & Warburg, London, 1934).

Martin Smith, *Burma: Insurgency and the Politics of Ethnicity* (Zed Books, London, 1991).

中国

INDEX

Americans
  in Burma, 152, 180
  in China, 88–89
Amnesty International, 154
An Australian in China
  (Morrison), 15–19, 20,
  113–14, 187–89
animism, 182–83
Aung San Suu Kyi, 163–64

Bai people, 112, *119*
Baidi Cheng, 56
Baoshan, 128, 133
Baptists, 182–83
Beijing, 61
Bell, Moberly, 15
Bhamo, 178–85
  at junction of rivers, 137
  Buddhist nuns in, *169*
  difficulty in entering,
  126, 127, 155, 158–59
  market, *172*
birds, setting free for
  merit, 162–63
bound feet, *79*
Boxer Rebellion, 15, 16, 19
bridges
  Rainbow Bridge,
  Shuizhai, 129, 130,
  132, *142*
  suspension bridges,
  132–33, 135, *142*, *144*
  Waibaidu Bridge,
  Shanghai, 23
  Xingxiu Bridge, Lufeng,
  106, *107*
British, in Burma, 137, 177
Buddhist nuns, *167*, *168*
Bund, The, Shanghai,
  23–30, *26–27*
Burma
  Aung San Suu Kyi,
  163–64
  Burma Road, 106, 137, 154
  Burmese Days, 178
  Chinese in, 174, 179–80
  difficulty in entering,
  126, 148, 155
  economy, 161–62
  Guomindang in, 151, 154
  massacre (1988), 161

official name change, 183n
self-imposed isolation, 20
see also Bhamo;
  Mandalay; Rangoon

Café de Jack, Dali, 113
Cangshan, 112
Catholics, 182
Chang Jiang, 47
Chiang Kai-shek, 32, 62
China Inland Mission, 116
China International
  Travel Service, 78
Chinese Communist
  Party, 19–20, 32
Chongqing, 14, 60–69,
  69–70, 88, 149
Christians, in China,
  113–16
Chungking, *see* Chongqing
CIA, 152
Cixi, 187
clothes, in China, 40
coal, *54*, 62
Communist Party of
  Burma, 136, 154, 174
Cultural Revolution, 47,
  90–91, 107–8
currency
  Burma, 158
  China, 17, 150
  Customs House,
  Shanghai, *26–27*, 29, 39

Daguan, 78–80
Daguanlou Grand
  Mansion, Kunming, *99*,
  103
Dali, 111–16, *117–23*
  Catholic Church, 150
  Church of Christ, 115–16
  Dali Lake, *120–21*
  heroin use in, 150–51
  Phoenix Eye Cave, 112
  Temple of Goddess of
  Mercy, 112, *118*
  views, *122*
  village market, *123*
dam project, Yangtze
  River, *see* Three Gorges
  Dam

Daojie, 133
Dashuijing, 84
Daying River, 137
Deng Xiaoping, 32, 59, 66
Dongfeng Hotel, 29
Dongfeng trucks, 128
door-gods, *76*
Dragon Lady, 16
drug addiction, 152–54
drug smuggling, 108
Du Wenxiu, 111
Du Yuesheng, 31, 32, 35
Dunn, Hugh, 13

'Eagle Nest Barrier', 109,
  117
Erhai Lake, *120–21*
Europeans, in China,
  18–19, 32–33

First Five Year Plan, 37
Fitzgerald, C.P., 131, 132
Five Foot Road, 17–18
floods, 47
Fort Dufferin, Mandalay,
  177
Franck, Harry, 34
funeral, near Burmese
  border, 138, *138*
Fu-to-kuan, 63–64

Gang of Four, 66, 108
Gezhou Dam, Yichang,
  48, 53
Gladney, Dru C., 107
Golden Triangle, 152, 154
Gongshan, *73*
Green Gang, 31, 32, 35
Guomindang, 19–20, 32,
  62, 151–52, 154

Han Chinese, 78, 134
Hanoi–Kunming railway, 82
Hanyang Ironworks,
  Wuhan, 45
Hard Rock Café, Dali, 111
heroin, 136, *146*, 151,
  152–54, 174
Hongkong & Shanghai
  Bank, Shanghai, *26–27*,
  29

Htay Aung, 159, 162,
  164–65
Huangpu Park, 29
Huangpu River, 23–24

Inya Lake, 163
Irrawaddy River, 137, *173*,
  175, *176*, 179

Jacob, Raymond, 12–13
Japanese
  in Burma, 177, 179, 182
  in China, 31, 63, 106, 133
Jensen, 16, 19, 86, 108
Jihong Bridge, *see* Rainbow
  Bridge, Shuizhai
Jinmasu, 90–91
Jinma pagoda, 91, *92–93*,
  102
Jinsha Jiang, 109
Jiong Qiao, *see* Rainbow
  Bridge, Shuizhai

Kachin Independence
  Army, 127, 139, 166,
  184, 186
Kachin people, 166, *181*,
  182–83
Karen people, 166, 182, 183
Kipling, Rudyard, 185
Kublai Khan, 102
Kulkarni, D.T., 13
Kunming, 86–104
  city wall, 87–88, *96–97*
  Morrison meets Jensen
  in, 19
  Muslim quarter, *94–95*,
  104
  pagoda at Jinmasu, 91,
  92–93
  temples, *99*, *100*
  views, *98*
Kuomintang, *see*
  Guomindang

Lancang Jiang, 128–29
Lesu people, 138
Liberation Monument,
  Chongqing, 61
Li Mi, 151, 152
Li Peng, 59

Lintner, Bertil, 151–52, 183
Liu Bei, 56
Liu's Café, Kunming, 87, 89
Lojie, 155
Long March, 103
Lufeng, Xingxiu Bridge, 106, *107*
Lyon, Albert J., 180

McDonald, Angus, *11, 143*
Manchu dynasty, *see* Qing dynasty
Mandalay, 173–78
  Hotel, 177
  Palace, *170–71*, 177
Mandalay Café, Tengchong, 135–36
Manyun, 137, 138
Mao suits, 40
Mao Zedong, 32, 39, 47, 66, 128
Mekong River, 128–29, *140–41*
missionaries
  Burma, 182–83
  China, 113–14
Missions Etrangères de Paris, Kunming, 89–91
Mong-Hsat, 151, 152
Morrison, Alastair, 20
Morrison, G.E., *3*
  accuracy of reporting questioned, 187
  almost drowns, 14
  biography, 13–15
  character, 16
  list of aims and achievements, 188–89
  map of journey, *189*
  meets Jensen in Kunming, 19
  on Chongqing, 62
  on Fu-to-kuan caves, 63–64
  on Lufeng stone bridge, 106
  on Mandalay, 174
  on missionaries, 113–14
  on Muslims in China, 108
  on opium-smokers, 148, 154
  on Rangoon, 163
  on Tengyueh, 137
  on the Americans in Burma, 180
  on Wuhan, 43
  provocation in Russo-Japanese War, 134

river trip to Mandalay, 185
  stays with Scottish missionary in Zhaotong, 81
  takes steamer to Wuhan, 39
  treatment of coolie, 149–50
Morrison Collection,
  Mitchell Library, 87, 89, 187
Morrison of Peking, 11, 20
Mount Everest, 12–13
Muslims, in China, *94–95*, 104, 107–8
Myanmar, *see* Burma
Myitkyina, 159, 165, 166
Myo Lwin, U, 126, 148, 155

Nanjing, 61, 63
Nanjing Road, Shanghai, *28*, 30
Nanking, *see* Nanjing
National League for Democracy, Burma, 164
Native of Beijing in New York, A, 83
Naw Taung, Paul, 180, 182, 184
nightclubs, Shanghai, 33–34
noodle-making, *95*

Olympic Games, 31–32
opium, 18–19, 31, *146*, 147–55, 174, 188n
Opium Wars, 19, 24
Orwell, George, 178

pagoda, at Jinmasu, 91, *92–93*, 102
Pearl, Cyril, 11, 13, 16, 187
Peking, *see* Beijing
People's Liberation Army, 108
Philp, Jon, 158–59
Phoenix Eye Cave, Dali, 112
Pinyin, 61
Pipa Shan, Chongqing, 66
pollution, in Chongqing, 62
Polo, Marco, 39, 102
prostitution, 34
Pupiao, 133

Qing dynasty, 18, 19, 45, 61, 82, 107
Qu Yuan, 55–56, 58–59

railways, 19
Rainbow Bridge, Shuizhai, 129, 130, 132, *142*
Rangoon, 90, 157–65, *163, 169*
Republican government, China, 19, 82
rickshaws, 174
Roberts Memorial Church, 180, 182
Roberts, William Henry, 180
Royal Commission on Opium, 149
Ruili, 155, 161
Russo-Japanese War, 134

St Ignatius Cathedral, Xujiahui, Shanghai, *25*, 35–36
Salween River, *125*, 137, *144*
Sandouping, 58
Scott, J.G., 174
Scott Market, Rangoon, 159, *160*, 161
Seagrave, Sterling, 16, 187
Shadian, 107–8
Shan people, 134, 138, 155
Shanghai, 8–10, 22–37
  Club, *26–27*, 29–30
  in 1894, 23
  Nanjing Road, *28*, 30
  nightclubs, 33–34
Shanyang, 128–29, 130
Shuizhai, 128–29
Shwe Dagon Pagoda, Rangoon, *156*, 162–63
Sichuan province, 63, 71
Sino-Japanese War, 133
Snow, Edgar, 63, 149
State Law and Order Restoration Council, Burma, 126, 139, 186
Suifu, 77
Sun Quan, 56
Sun Ranweng, 103
suspension bridges, 132–33, 135, *142, 144*

tai chi, *100*
Tai people, 134
Taiping Rebellion, 43
Taiwan, 152
Taiwo (ship), 39
Tali, *see* Dali
Tatmadaw, 177, 178
tea-carriers, *76*

telegraph installation, 19
television, 83
Tengchong, 135–37, 139, *145*, 161
textiles, 45
Thibaw, King, 177, 180
Three Gorges Dam project, 48, 54, 58–59
Tianshentang, 109–11
Times, The, 15, 16, 187
tobacco, 81
Treaty of Tientsin, 113
Tuan Shi-wen, 152

Waibaidu Bridge, Shanghai, 23
weddings, *101*, 179–80
World War II, 62–63
Wuchidao, 17–18
Wudi, 134
Wuhan, *28*, 43–45, 63
Wu Yung Sen, *105*

Xia Guan, 127, 154
Xiling Gorge, 56
Xingxiu Bridge, Lufeng, 106, *107*
Xinjiang, 108

Yangtze Gorges, 14, *46*, *50–51*, *52*, 56–58
Yangtze River
  boats on, *38, 49*
  geography, 46–47
  steamer voyage up, 39–45
Yibin, 77
Yichang, 48, 54, 56–57
Yingwuguan, 108–10, *117*
Yingyiang, 137, 138
Yi people, 108
Yuan Shikai, 83
Yuantong Temple, Kunming, *100*
Yunnan City, *see* Kunming
Yunnan–Guizhou Tableland, 18, 82
Yunnan province, 18, 78–85, 149

Zar Chi Win Hotel, Rangoon, 158
Zhaotong, *72–73*, 80–81, 83–84
Zhou Enlai, 31, 32
Zhuge Liang, 56, 132
Zigui, 58

中国

萬曆府縣全圖